GENERAL MAXIME WEYGAND, 1867–1965

ANTHONY CLAYTON

GENERAL MAXIME WEYGAND

⚔ 1867-1965

FORTUNE AND MISFORTUNE

INDIANA UNIVERSITY PRESS *Bloomington & Indianapolis*

This book is a publication of

INDIANA UNIVERSITY PRESS
Office of Scholarly Publishing
Herman B Wells Library 350
1320 East 10th Street
Bloomington, Indiana 47405 USA

iupress.indiana.edu

∞ The paper used in this publication meets the minimum
requirements of the American National Standard for Information
Sciences—Permanence of Paper for Printed Library Materials,
ANSI Z39.48–1992.

Manufactured in the United States of America

Library of Congress Cataloging-in-Publication Data

Clayton, Anthony, [date]
  General Maxime Weygand, 1867–1965 : fortune and misfortune / Anthony Clayton.
    pages cm
  Includes bibliographical references and index.
  ISBN 978-0-253-01582-2 (cloth : alk. paper) — ISBN 978-0-253-01585-3 (ebook) 1. Weygand,
Maxime, 1867–1965. 2. Generals—France—Biography. 3. France. Armée—Officers—
Biography. 4. World War, 1939–1945—Campaigns—France. 5. World War, 1939–1945—
Campaigns—Africa, North. I. Title.
  DC373.W4C53 2015
  355.0092—dc23
  [B]
                          2014029045

1 2 3 4 5 20 19 18 17 16 15

In the summer of 1920, in
the Polish capital city, Warsaw,
a French officer and a British officer
worked closely together for a common good.
The personality of the French officer left its mark
on his British colleague. Almost a century later,
a by-product was to be this work.

The British officer was this author's father.

CONTENTS

Preface and Acknowledgments   ix

1 Birth and Early Years, 1867–1914   3

2 Chief of Staff, 1914–18   14

3 Versailles, Warsaw, Syria, 1919–24   45

4 Defense Policy in a Fractured France, 1925–39   55

5 Commander in Chief, May–June 1940   77

6 Minister for National Defense, June–September 1940   102

7 A General Out of Step: North Africa, 1940–41   115

8 Final Misfortunes and Final Years, 1941–65   128

Notes   143
Selected Bibliography   153
Index   157

PREFACE AND ACKNOWLEDGMENTS

General Maxime de Nimal Weygand lived an extraordinary life, achieving a pinnacle of fame and prestige, but then later finding himself, in the words of Shakespeare's Rosalind, "out of suits with fortune," a life that presents a challenge to any biographer.

From the circumstances of his birth to the arrangements for his funeral Weygand aroused controversy. After an outstanding First World War career as chief of staff for Marshal Foch and service after the war in Poland and Syria, Weygand became increasingly alarmed by the accession to power of the Nazis in Germany and German rearmament. As a national figure of great prestige and until 1935 France's senior soldier, Weygand had to face the first of two of the most difficult decisions that could confront an army commander in peacetime: what should he do when faced with a clear and highly dangerous military threat likely to bring catastrophe upon his country when the civilian political leadership largely chose to deny the threat? Weygand's concerns over the state of the French army, concerns also expressed by some right-wing groups, led to accusations that he was anti-democratic. He always personally disassociated himself from the political activities of these groups, but the accusations were to reappear after the end of the Second World War.

Summoned to be commander in chief in mid-May 1940, Weygand was very quickly faced with his second and even more difficult decision: what does an army commander do when before him lies a crushing military defeat not of his own making but bringing with it heavy bloodshed of his soldiers and appalling civilian suffering? Weygand's battle plans to meet the German invasion were as sound as any could be in this situation, but with total defeat only a few days away he almost violently imposed his will on the French prime minister, shouting against proposals for a complete surrender and laying down of arms (and for allowing the government to depart into a secure ease). Instead, Weygand sought an armistice in order to save military and civilian lives and to provide a period of truce during which France might rebuild capability for a later return to the war.

The post-armistice Vichy government headed by Marshal Pétain, at that time still held in high regard, was hugely popular with the French public. At its outset Weygand had every reason, political and constitutional, for considering it a legitimate government. Weygand was sent to North Africa with full vice regal powers in October 1940 and spent a year there covertly laying the foundations for an army to rejoin the Allied cause, as later "*l'Armée de Weygand*" was to do in Tunisia, in Italy, and in the Liberation campaigns. He also initiated economic and intelligence relationships with the United States. Weygand was totally opposed to the views gaining strength in Vichy that a German victory was inevitable and that French interests were best secured by association with the Germans as a loyal junior partner. His opposition to these views, vigorously expressed, led to his dismissal in November 1941. These twelve months in service to Pétain and the Vichy government unfortunately established the grounds for his vendetta with Charles de Gaulle in London.

In the final Vichy years when occurred the regime's worst excesses—the fascist-style militia and the dispatch of Jewish men women and children to extermination camps—Weygand was no longer in office. After the German entry into Unoccupied France, he was arrested by the Germans, remaining in prison for the rest of the war. He was released in May 1945, only to be immediately rearrested in Paris on the orders of de Gaulle. In the climate of the Liberation, de Gaulle and the Resistance were presented as the only paths of honor, and any senior figure who had served Vichy was considered to have been dishonorable and probably treacherous. Pétain himself was tried and imprisoned for life. After lengthy and controversial court proceedings and inquiries, Weygand was acquitted of the charges brought against him, the court ruling that he had never acted against the interests of France. His honors—and full pension—were restored to him. However, at his death in 1965 when de Gaulle was president of the Republic, Weygand was deprived of the honor of a military funeral. Despite this ban, a very large number of wartime generals and other officers were present for the funeral service at a parish church in Paris.

In consideration of this turbulent life two other issues personal to Weygand merit mention. The first is the old military cliché that good staff officers do not make good commanders. Weygand's battlefield decisions in 1940 have been criticized, but there is little reason to suggest any were wrong, and strong arguments can be made that they were the best and most honorable options open to him. The second issue is whether any tensions arising from his origins affected the decisions that he had to make. There is certainly evidence that internal tensions, in a man whose temperament was more soldierly than patient, appeared in explosions of temper at moments of exasperation. But these were no worse than outbursts by many other generals, French—and American. There is no case here for psychohistory.

The writer of a historical biography must try to know and to understand the historical contexts, sometimes deep or at other times dramatically changing, in which the subject had to act. He or she must know the details of the subject's actions and their impacts and must analyze the motivations for these actions—a difficult task as motivations are not always what either the subject or the subject's critics assert. Motivations can be affected by birth, upbringing in a particular culture and society, the pattern of career development, religious and ideological beliefs, devotion to an institution, psychological props such as service in the navy or army, personal affairs, and temperaments and physical heath; sometimes these may be subconscious. Attempts to contain an unpleasant factor or memory can be seen as dutiful, self-sacrificing, and at least stoic if not particularly heroic. But such containment can create fresh tensions, possibly resentful or aggressive, which can in turn lead to action, fatalistic inaction, or simply a wrong decision seen as being for the right reasons. A biographer must be on guard. Such internal tensions may exist or the biographer may be simply imagining or exaggerating their existence as a result of his or her own personal preconceptions. In this work on Weygand, I have sought to keep these considerations to the fore in my mind.

Earlier works on Weygand present very different points of view. Weygand's first biographer, Bernard Destremau, writes the life of a patriot who from 1919 onward argued fiercely but in vain for proper armament, security, and an effective professional army. Destremau is, however, at times selective of facts and generally uncritical. Philip Bankwitz writes from a traditional liberal-democratic view of civil-military relations. He claims that Weygand's arguments, particularly in the 1930s, were malignant and counterproductive, widening distrust between political leaders and the military, all a psychological preparation for the disaster and the authoritarianism of the Vichy era. For these consequences Weygand, at the critical moment finally flouting the authority of his prime minister, must bear responsibility, a severe historical judgment, but one too narrow to be final.

This work will offer a third, very different and more historically based analysis, seeing the defeat in 1940 as a tragic but ongoing consequence of the deep fault line of suspicion, distrust, at times hatred opened in French society by the violence of the French 1789 Revolution. The depth of this fault line reappeared in the extreme violence by both sides in the 1871 Paris Commune, the distrust of the military in the twentieth-century *Affaire des Fiches,* the passions aroused by the Dreyfus affair, and the controversies over defense in the 1930s. Fundamental perceptions of what constituted a security policy, involving as they did the whole concept and very existence of a professional army, were irreconcilable and became bitter. The resulting inability of minds to meet, minds formed by history into two totally opposing traditions, led inexorably to the French collapse of May–June 1940. Weygand did not write this historical script or any part of it. He was merely a lead actor in the inevitable tragedy.

The works of Destremau and Bankwitz, together with a very popular style biography by Barnett Singer, are all well based on detailed research. This work fully and freely acknowledges my great indebtedness to them, their research, and their sources. But a reappraisal of Weygand's life with a different argument is certainly now permissible. I have attempted to achieve this with a wider revisionary consideration of the facts in these works and from other sources.

This work could never have been written and produced without the assistance of several kind and very long suffering helpers. First and foremost Gillian James, an old friend and colleague from Surrey University days who has managed to make sense out of my spidery scrawl and numerous additions to the first draft of my manuscript and convert it to typescript—a heroic achievement. Andrew Orgill and his colleagues at the Library of the Royal Military Academy Sandhurst, John Pearce and Ken Franklin, have provided not only professional help but great encouragement. The Sandhurst Library is a very special place, much loved by its users, military and academic. A friend of many years' standing and of teaching days at Sandhurst before we both reached pension-grade age, Dr. Ned Willmott has helped me timelessly with transport of myself and books to and from my home to the Academy. John Card's technical knowledge of electronic communication has had to fill in for my own total lack of such knowledge. I was ejected from my school's physics class as hopeless; the history teacher felt that he could take a more kindly view.

Across the Channel I owe a debt of gratitude to my friend and colleague M. Jose Maigre, military historian and former librarian at the French army's officer cadet academy at Saint-Cyr-Coëtquidan, for useful advice.

GENERAL MAXIME WEYGAND, 1867–1965

Born in 1867, parents unknown;
In 1914–18 a chief of staff;
In 1940 a commander in chief;
In 1941 a general out of step with the Vichy regime;
In 1942–45 arrested, placed in German, then French, detention;
In 1949 honors restored;
Died in 1965, denied military funeral.

1

⸗+ ⸗+ ⸗+

BIRTH AND EARLY YEARS
1867–1914

Few general officers commanding a nation's army have had no certain knowledge of the identity or even the nationality of either of their parents or of the place of their birth. The baby later known to the world as Maxime Weygand was registered as having been born on January 21, 1867. A certificate of birth dated the 23rd records the birth as having taken place at Brussels and notes the infant's name only as Maxime. The birth certificate does not record the names of the parents and gives the place of birth as a room above a storehouse, 39 Boulevard de Waterloo, Brussels. Both the date and the place of birth are open to question. The doctor had a questionable record, and the witnesses were illiterate. Post-1945 inquiries only indicated that neither the storekeeper nor the owner of the property knew anything of the infant's parentage, and no trace remained of the two witnesses.

Weygand's biographer, Bernard Destremau, offers five possible pairs of candidates and examines the case for each in some detail.[1] The first pairing, Leopold II, king of the Belgians, and either the wife of Count Zichy, an Austrian diplomat, or an anonymous Mexican woman, raises serious doubts. Although generous with his favors, Leopold had at the time other interests, and as an adult Weygand bore no resemblance whatsoever to Leopold in either appearance or character. The argument that Leopold was the father, was, however, later to prove popular in France and was believed by many French officers of Roman Catholic and closet royalist beliefs. The second possibility, a liaison between Charlotte, the

3

wife of Archduke Maximilian of Austria, at the time briefly emperor
of Mexico, and a Belgian colonel named van der Smissen, at the time
serving in Mexico, is even less probable inasmuch as concealment of an
empress's pregnancy would have been almost impossible. Least probable
of all is a liaison between Weygand's boyhood tutor, a Belgian of Spanish
origin named David Cohen, and a French woman originally of Belgian
nationality, Thérèse Denimal. Their claim attracts interest in Belgium but
lacks credibility. Hardly more probable is a relationship between, again,
Charlotte, empress of Mexico, and a Mexican, either a medical friend or
a Colonel Lopez; again such a relationship would have been difficult to
hide. Most likely, but not certain, is that the infant was the product of life
in the louche, Vienna-style imperial court at Chapultepec in Mexico, of an
affaire between Maximilian himself and a strikingly beautiful Mexican
dancer known variously as Guadelupe Martinez, Lupe, or La Belle Indi-
enne. According to this argument the baby was born either in Mexico or
elsewhere and was carried by Guadelupe in the early stages of her pregnancy when she may have been a maid of honor for the Empress Charlotte.
By this theory the Brussels birth documents were prepared by a compli-
ant doctor, following the pleadings of Charlotte, who had not been able
to produce a child herself, to her brother King Leopold—Maximilian's
father Francis-Joseph, the emperor of Austria, being unwilling to help.
Whatever the truth, Guadelupe conveniently disappeared or was paid
off soon after the birth.

There are strong arguments to support this last scenario, however
elaborate. Weygand himself was short in stature, five feet seven inches
in height, and his rounded facial appearance and sallow complexion suggest a non-European or partly European parentage. Later Weygand was
often called "le petit général jaune" by French officers. The name of the
baby, Maxime, may also provide a clue. Francis-Joseph was on good terms
with his Belgian brother-in-law. Some secret arrangement for irregular
payments for the boy's upbringing and later military career undoubtedly
existed.[2] The secrecies were perpetuated by the assassination of Maximilian at the hands of Mexican rebels and the disappearance of Guadelupe,
neither possible parent remaining to tell a tale. The suicide of Francis-
Joseph's heir, Rudolf, with his mistress at Mayerling in 1889 opened a
fear in Francis-Joseph that an illegitimate Mexican might lay claim to the

Habsburg throne, an additional reason for economy with the truth. On his deathbed Weygand repeated earlier statements that he did not know who his parents were or his place of birth. It is, however, not unreasonable to suggest that as he grew older he might have been increasingly aware of the moneys made available for, and later paid directly, to him, and drawn conclusions, but if so he then decided it best for all concerned to keep them to himself. The truth will never be known, but much later in his life, in 1940, these doubts were to make some decision-making embarrassing for him, though it is very doubtful if they were ever a factor with respect to any specific issue. These doubts surrounding his parentage did undoubtedly contribute to his later views on strict order, fixed procedures, and government legitimacy. These views found reinforcement in his firm belief in the truths and hierarchies of the Roman Catholic faith. Nevertheless, this attempt to build an orderly structure on the uncertain foundation of his birth could not protect him from the deprecations of his critics, particularly after the fall of France, who dismissed him because "of course, he was not born a Frenchman."

Details of the little boy's life and upbringing are few and confusing.[3] Known simply as Maxime, he was taken to France, initially to Marseille, soon after his birth. Those immediately in charge of him were anxious to be free of him and assumed fewer questions were likely to be asked in France than in Belgium or Austria. At Marseilles, Maxime was placed in the care of Madame Saget, a nurse. The future general recalled being addressed as Maxime Saget. Madame Saget was very strict; the boy had corporal punishment rather than affection. In 1874, in order to meet French legal requirements, the seven-year-old boy was placed in the care of a Marseille leather merchant, David Cohen, who served as Maxime's tutor, and his partner Thérèse Denimal. To improve their own and the boy's social status they altered their names. Cohen, a Belgian born in Italy, claimed Spanish nationality and took the name de Leon; his partner rose to the minor nobility by simply changing Denimal to de Nimal. Her name was given to the boy and he remained Maxime de Nimal until he was commissioned into the French Army in 1888. The pair enrolled Maxime in a school at Cannes, and then another at Asniéres, where it seems he was mocked for having no parents. At the same time it was noted that he was a very bright pupil. While David and Thérèse looked after the boy's scholastic development, theirs was a relationship lacking in affection. Maxime had yet to find a family.

It is not known whether any provision had been made for Maxime's financial support. No details survive; only surmise is possible. The probability remains that money came from Belgium, from either the government, the royal household, or a charity with royal patronage, but if this support existed at all it must have been very modest since it is clear that the boy's daily life was one of near-poverty. It is possible that Maxime's fees for schools, lycée, and later Saint-Cyr were paid by others, and he may have received money for his marriage. All that can be said with certainty is that some moneys arrived sometimes.

In 1875, when he was ten, it was decided that the boy should go to a boarding school in Paris. He was first sent to a suburban school in Vanves and then in 1881 to the Lycée Louis-le-Grand, at the time one of the finest schools in France. While at Vanves he read Corneille's classic play *Le Cid* and was impressed with its patriotic nationalist soldier hero. Despite the fact that the school was ostensibly secular, and the climate of the time anticlerical, Maxime was baptized. The conversion was the work of a priest, Abbé de Bonfils, who acted as the school chaplain, an appointment still at the time permitted. De Bonfils noted both Maxime's ability and his loneliness, and the jibes he suffered about having no parents, which were particularly acute on days when parents arrived to take their boys out. The abbé carefully built up the boy's self-confidence, and he also counseled the young de Nimal to curb his exceedingly violent temper. With this he achieved only partial success; Maxime's temper remained explosive all his life.

Becoming a Roman Catholic with the Church's order, discipline, and certainties of faith gave the boy for the first time some sense of direction and belonging, over and above the chaos of his life to that time. All his life Weygand remained a strict, devout Catholic, his beliefs frequently arousing controversy.

Life at the Lycée Louis-le-Grand was a Spartan regime of petty authority, cold water and rooms, and unappetizing food. While local Paris boys enjoyed treats, the young de Nimal in his early teenage years was left lonely and miserable. In March 1883 a revolt of the pupils broke out. Maxime was one of the instigators; in his case the revolt was an expression of the pent-up repression that he had suffered in his early years, fueled by his explosive temper. Rioting spread to his dormitory, where de Nimal organized a defense with bedsteads and *paillasses*. The police were needed to restore order. De Nimal was unceremoniously expelled and banned from admission to any other school in Paris. The experience chastened the boy. Recalling Abbé de Bonfil's teaching, he accepted his expulsion as a lesson learned for life and realized his need for an earthly guiding authority as well as an inner spiritual one.

After some special pleading, the young de Nimal was accepted as a pupil at a lycée of indifferent quality in Toulon. There he attempted to rebuild his fortunes, working extremely hard. He was moved to a much better lycée in Aix en Provence, where he passed the first part of his *baccalauréat*. He passed the second part in Paris, following this success with a science course at the Lycée Henri IV. Learning from his Louis-le-Grand experience, he had become a more moderate young man, and for the first time in his life he began to make friends. At the time he considered joining the French Navy and went to sea on board a training ship. Unfortunately, his unruly habits and disdain for discipline reappeared, and the navy said that they did not want him. The army was suggested as an alternative.

Maxime had earlier been attracted to the army; the national school syllabus spoke of the need to recover Alsace and Lorraine, and extolled military virtues. He immediately began preparing for his entry to the Saint-Cyr military cadet academy. As a Belgian he could have entered Saint-Cyr without taking the stiff French entrance examinations. His ambition was to be a French officer, so much to his credit he set himself to the task of preparation in the same way as French candidates. David Cohen indicated willingness to pay fees, though one may suspect with continued covert assistance from Belgium as Cohen's business interests were not very successful. A local Marseille politician, Maurice Rouvier, smoothed the way with other formalities, particularly those of parentage and a necessary authorization from the minister for war that had to be arranged. Later when de Nimal had been accepted, the touchy subject of uniform arose. The Saint-Cyr authorities at first denied him the French uniform, eventually conceding the uniform but without rank badges, a slight that Maxime resented.

He passed the entrance examination 58th (later amended to 20th) out of 394 applicants. He performed well at Saint-Cyr, passing out among the top ten. The mentally and physically challenging routine suited him well; he later described it as a "sort of deliverance." At Saint-Cyr he also distinguished himself in fencing and more importantly as an outstanding horseman. These accomplishments gave him a social pass to a circle of future cavalry officers from "established families," and led him on to his first posting after graduation. Still known as de Nimal, he was accepted for a further young officers' course at the cavalry school at Saumur. There he passed 9th out of a group of 78 young officers, but then to his fury he was told that as a foreigner he could serve only in the Foreign Legion. Cohen and the Aix-en-Provence politician Rouvier again came to the rescue, finding a man, Rouvier's accountant, prepared to consider adopting Sous-Lieutenant Maxime de Nimal as his son. This kindly man was Francis-Joseph Weygand, a widower with a small daughter, at the time living in Arras but also a former citizen of Strasbourg in German-occupied Alsace, which raised further nationality complications. Eventually, after much hesitation and some transactions with Cohen, Weygand agreed. And on October 18, 1888 the young cavalry subaltern Maxime de Nimal Weygand was posted to the 4e Régiment de Dragons at Chambéry.

This remarkable ascent from unwanted illegitimate orphan to officer in a smart cavalry regiment provided Weygand with the second of his essential character-forming beliefs—the importance of order, authority and hierarchy, patriotism and discipline. These beliefs as he understood them, together with his Catholic faith, were to remain the lodestars that he followed with fervor for the rest of his life and that governed his actions at all times.

The army that Weygand was joining was not a happy one.[4] It was poorly paid and underresourced. Its defeat, despite some epic encounters, in the Franco-Prussian War (1870–71) had left an atmosphere of sullen revanchism. Many of its officers were from the traditional "establishment," overtly or covertly monarchist, disliking or despising the noisy anticlerical politics active in the newly formed Third Republic. The sudden exposure in 1889 of the populist pro-Republic General Georges Boulanger as a man of straw, capable only of indecision, flight, and suicide, further damaged the army's image. Worse was to follow.

In 1894 the long-running and bitterly divisive Dreyfus case opened with espionage charges against Captain Alfred Dreyfus, a general staff officer of Jewish origin. On forged evidence Dreyfus was convicted, disgraced, and imprisoned. There followed over the next years mounting political and often press criticism that, together with the work of an honest staff officer within the army, led to a national quest for justice. The conservative army officers reacted strongly, arguing that the criticism was the work of Jews, Freemasons, and the Germans and a slur on the honor of the army. The honest officer was dismissed. But in time public pressure and further investigation exposed the false nature of the evidence upon which the conviction was based, the later distortions and deliberate manufacture of false evidence used to justify them, and the identity of the real offender. The whole scandal became public knowledge, and after long and severe prison sentences Dreyfus was finally restored to his rank in 1906. The traditional leadership of the army emerged as decoupled from the state, anti-Semitic, and a danger to the Republic. The entire incident is perhaps best seen as another opening up of the divisive fault lines in French national life caused by the abuses of the ancien regime and the violence and excesses of the Revolution.

One of the consequences of the Dreyfus case was the anti-Catholic policy of the 1902 Emile Combes government, which aimed at ensuring that all senior civil and military appointments were filled by true secular Republicans. The policy would prove to be even more divisive, both within the army and for the army as a state institution. Combes's war minister, Republican General Louis André, ordered officers to teach Republican values and assist in the closure of certain anti-Dreyfusard religious institutions. Officers who could combine Republician with anti-Dreyfusard conservative views were selected for accelerated promotion; those of known Catholic views passed over, among them Weygand's future chief, Ferdinand Foch. Republican officers were used to spy on their Catholic contemporaries, opening files and *fiches,* and recording their habits, such as eating only fish on Fridays. *Aumôniers,* chaplains, were phased out. The line infantry and cavalry, which contained majorities of traditionally minded French officers, especially suffered. Logistics officers with anti-Catholic views received preference.

The Combes government fell in 1906, but much damage had been done, and the deployment of troops to contain industrial unrest in 1905, 1907, and 1911 did nothing to improve matters. The apparent growing menace of the German Empire in some measure served to concentrate minds and overcome differences, but there were still numerous voices on the political left calling for a nonprofessional national guard citizen army, arguing that *liberté, égalité, fraternité* had been replaced with *infanterie, artillerie, cavalerie,* all dominated by a reactionary officer caste.

The beginning of the 1914–18 war found the army generally in good morale but underresourced, short of officers and good noncommissioned officers, with a number of conscripts only half-trained and reservists recalled to duty, most but not all of whom demonstrated the widely publicized enthusiasm. Strategic thinking was based on a concept of victory by means of attack, to be so vigorous and so long sustained as to be irresistible. Equipment ranging from the bright colors of uniforms thought to provide inspiration in battle to the flat trajectory of the otherwise excellent 75mm field gun, and the disbelief in the need for defensive weaponry such as machine guns, were all part of the thinking. To all this was added Plan 17, which envisaged a major three-army opening offensive action in Lorraine and Alsace. Its designers either ignored the many clear indicators warning of the German Schlieffen plan to seize Paris by an encircling sweep through Belgium or believed that Plan 17 would be so successful that it would negate any German gains elsewhere. Disasters were soon to follow.

For Weygand the years from 1888 to 1914 saw steady career advancement from subaltern to lieutenant colonel within the closed world of a cavalry regimental officer. He lived the life of a young cavalry officer to the full. He was an excellent horseman, a social success in the different garrison-town high societies at his various postings (these were frequent in French cavalry at this time), and popular with his brother officers and his NCOs. The officers were ordered not to ask questions about his family or the source of his occasional private income that he spent at equestrian events. His brother officers assumed he was the illegitimate son of the king of the Belgians, giving him a certain cachet. The ethos of cavalry regiments was in any case antiacademic, limited to debate about setting a social tone, centering upon horses and women; the dapper young Weygand proved as much a success with the latter as with the former. His personal style was gentlemanly, aristocratic, with no pretentions to royalty. He took only a passing interest in the Dreyfus affair, considering Dreyfus to have been guilty and subscribing to a fund for the widow of the staff officer,

Major Henry, who had prepared the forged document. He was officially reprimanded by the war minister, Freycinet, and given four days of arrest.[5] He was fortunate enough to have escaped notice in the *fiches* affair, being almost certainly too junior.

Marriage was expected of officers after a few years' service.[6] For many in the cavalry, aristocratic relatives with attractive daughters were generally around, but this was not the case for Weygand, nor did he have a solid estate. It seems that in 1900 mutual attraction drew him to the daughter of his colonel, the attractive Marie-Renée Jocélane de Forsanz. Renée, twenty-three years old and very intelligent, was determined to make her own choice. Her father, soon promoted to general, liked and respected Weygand and was delighted at first. But others soon began to raise doubts—who was this man with no family? The general's aristocratic Polish mother-in-law also objected. The general and his wife traveled to Marseille to try to find out more, but learned nothing other than tittle-tattle. They then went to Brussels, returning to proclaim that they had been advised their future son-in-law came from an excellent family; the adviser was not named.

On November 13, 1900, the couple was married in Noyon Cathedral, returning to live in the Paris suburb of Vannes. A month earlier the name on the bridegroom's birth certificate had been changed from de Nimal to Weygand. His marriage into an established family was the final stage of the rebranding of the orphan Maxime into a confident French cavalry officer and gentleman. The marriage was a happy one; two sons followed quickly. With achievement and a family, Weygand matured. He began reading widely and was increasingly interested in the arts. Renée loyally soothed any doubts, conscious or subconscious, that Weygand may have had about his origins, and the couple was very popular socially, as both hosts and guests.

Seen as a promising young cavalry officer, Weygand was again posted to the instructor's course at the cavalry school at Saumur from which he passed out first. He stayed on as an instructor at Saumur until 1907. He was regarded as an exceptional instructor, inspiring his students by his teaching, but it seems that by 1907 Weygand was dissatisfied with the teaching of the traditional roles of the cavalry, reconnaissance, flank cover, pursuit, and above all the charge. He studied the Russo-Japanese

War of 1904–1905, especially the Battle of Mukden, and noted the power of the new weapon, the machine gun. His success at Saumur spared him from the necessity of attending the Ecole de Guerre, normally essential for career prospects, and after two years' service with the 7ᵉ Hussars he returned to Saumur for a further two years. Promotion for him was unusually rapid for the time; he became a captain in 1896, major in 1907, and lieutenant colonel in 1912.[7]

In that year Weygand was accepted for the higher staff course referred to as the course for future marshals at the Centre des Hautes Etudes Militaires, where he was instructed in interarms cooperation and staff work. He was seen as outstanding, attracting the notice of General Joseph Joffre, who was to become the French Army commander in chief in August 1914. Joffre asked Weygand what would be his ambition in time of war, to which Weygand answered that it would be the command of a cavalry regiment. Joffre responded, "In the name of God we did not bring you here for that."

After a return to another regiment, the 5ᵉ Hussars, as a staff officer, Weygand received a sudden order to be part of a mission to Russia, with Joffre as head of the mission. The mission was received by the tsar and the Grand Duke Nicholas, the Russian Army's commander in chief designate. Watching the army's maneuvers, Weygand was impressed by the more practical mild-green colors of the soldiers' uniforms and the artillery's telephone communication systems, but he was very much aware of Russia's poor railway communications and supported the plans for French loans to hasten railroad development. Carried through, these plans would have greatly reduced the nineteen days of mobilization that the Russian Army required to prepare for an attack, but the completion date envisaged, 1918, was to prove unrealistic. Weygand also found the alcoholic intake of Russian officers at receptions to be excessive. After the mission was over, Lieutenant Colonel Weygand returned to his regiment at Nancy. On three occasions in early 1914 he met briefly with General Foch at conferences or on maneuvers.

In contrast with the Russian officers, Weygand had kept himself fully fit with daily exercise, riding, and swimming. (Others of his promotion intake at Saint-Cyr had allowed themselves to put on weight and were referred to as "the Senators.") As the war clouds gathered, his chief concern was the hurried exit, in the event on the last train, of his wife and elder son, Edouard, who were at the time living in Germany, where the boy was learning German.

On July 28, 1914, the 5ᵉ Hussars men on leave were recalled and the regiment moved to the frontier. After war was declared by Germany on August 3, the 5ᵉ Hussars, part of General Foch's XX Corps, engaged in several brushes with the Germans during the bloody Battle of Morhange. Elsewhere the French Army was soon in difficulties as the Germans swept through Belgium. Joffre decided to form a new Ninth Army from the XX Corps with Foch as its commander. On the 17th two officers were ordered by Joffre to report to Foch for staff duties with the new army. Foch asked which of the two was the older, a question to which he already knew the answer. Despite the fact that technically the other officer was the senior, Weygand was able to reply that he was the older. The reasons behind Foch's question will never be known; the probability is that at some time earlier Joffre had commented to Foch on Weygand's capabilities, which he had seen demonstrated at the Centre and in Russia.[8] There is also the possibility that one of Joffre's operations staff officers, Captain Maurice Gamelin, may have had an input. Weygand's French biographer, however, believes it was a simple choice. Foch urgently needed a chief of staff and opted for the older man with the view that if he was inadequate he could be dismissed and replaced very quickly. Whatever the reasons, Maxime Weygand now found himself chief of staff to a general who was to prove the greatest French commander in the four-year-long war. His first moment of destiny had arrived.

2

⊨ ⊨ ⊨

CHIEF OF STAFF
1914–18

Staffs exist to support commanders in their duties in peace and war.
Throughout the nineteenth century warfare had become infinitely more
complex and commanders more and more dependent on trained staffs.
Countries opened army staff colleges. Different countries chose different approaches to create the best structure for staffs. The British Army,
for example, preferred commanders, at any level between a brigade and
an army corps, to have two officers in charge of staffs and staff work, one
for operations and intelligence, the other for personnel and supply; these
officers were equal in badged rank but with the former generally the senior. At army level, personnel and supply were separated, a third senior
staff officer being necessary. The French preference had evolved into one
that divided staff work into three main bureaus: first, supply, logistics,
and administration; second, intelligence; and third, operations, all under
a chief of staff. This structure had to be considerably modified as the First
World War developed, when a fourth bureau for logistics was set up in 1917.

Whatever the structure, it is useful to set out the basic support a general
from brigade to army levels would expect from his staff in the circumstances of the Western Front, mobile fighting in 1914 and in 1918 but static
from 1915 to early 1918.

The first item of support—and it may seem not the most important but
could matter a great deal—was accommodation and personal facilities
where the commanding general would live, eat, rest, and think, which
would permit him to move to any section of the front that he might wish

to visit; where he would hold meetings; and which would include sufficient staff for communication by radio, landline, horse dispatch riders and motorcycle dispatch riders, liaison officers, and at times even the humble pigeon for the all-important communication between headquarters, regiments, and flanking headquarters.

The second support necessity was intelligence staff operators to collect raw information from all the possible sources: infantry observation posts and patrols discerning enemy trench unit identities, trench lines and mine-laying, ongoing machine gun and field artillery gun positions; the questioning of prisoners, deserters, and refugees; the study of captured documents, reports from air observation and photography, artillery intelligence about the source, direction, and nature of enemy fire, and material from higher formations ranging from enemy troop railway movements to assessed capabilities of new enemy weaponry. This mass of information had to be collated, analyzed, and presented clearly and objectively at a time, often immediate, when it was required.[1]

Third were the operations staff, who had to be ready to inform the commander on the immediate state of battle involving frontline units and any changes, advance, or withdrawal, as well as the enemy's apparent frontline objectives; casualties; and the location where reinforcements or artillery support was necessary—all together with a second major duty, the preparation of plans for intended projects that had been ordered or for sudden emergencies, maintenance of military war diaries and records, and the provision of reports and casualty rolls.

Fourth, staff for the logistics of the battle, ammunition and food, transport, special equipment that might be needed for a particular project; provision for the wounded and the holding of prisoners; fodder for horses or mules and fuel for petrol-engine transport; relief and rest arrangements for regiments between tours of duty in the frontline trenches; postal arrangements; and in the case of the French Army, the censoring of letters, which were seen as very important indicators of the state of morale.

In the French Army the overall responsibility for ensuring that all these vitally important functions were at full efficiency fell to the formation's chief of staff. The requisite personal relationship or bond between a chief of staff and his generals was never set out and was impossible to define. Some generals treated their chiefs as mere executives; others made

it clear that the major decisions fell to themselves but would discuss projects with their chiefs of staff prior to detailed planning. Sometimes the
chief of staff would be a general's sounding board. In a few cases the overall field commander was not capable of fulfilling the role or was simply a
political nominee, and his chief of staff was the formation commander
in all but name. Very occasionally backgrounds, beliefs, and personal
chemistry could produce such a partnership between commanding generals and chiefs of staff that they spoke as one person. Such was to be the
partnership now to begin between General Foch and Lieutenant Colonel
Weygand.

In August 1914 few would have predicted either that the war would last
four years or that General Foch, then commanding an army corps, would
emerge to be his nation's foremost soldier. Ferdinand Foch was the son of a
minor civil servant, and was born in 1851 in the Pyrenees town of Tarbes.
His family had a military tradition dating back to the Napoleonic era.
Foch joined the infantry in 1870 but did not see any actual fighting in the
Franco-Prussian War. A gifted officer, he was able to enter the prestigious
Ecole Polytechnique, from which, now more scientifically trained, he became an artilleryman serving in a number of regiments before entering
the Ecole de Guerre in 1885. After a staff appointment Foch was selected
in 1890 to serve in the elite Third Bureau, Operations, of the General
Staff, where he served for two years, with a further year in 1894, before
returning to the Ecole de Guerre in 1896, being then promoted to the pro-
fessorship of military history, strategy, and tactics. In 1901, posted to an
artillery regiment, he fell victim to the anticlerical prejudices of the time
and received no further promotion until 1903, when he became a colonel
with the command of a regiment. In 1907 he became brigadier general.
The following year, having gone to great lengths to convince the prime
minister, the anticlerical Georges Clemenceau, that he was a reliable Republican, he became commandant of the Ecole de Guerre. At the Guerre
Foch changed the rank of students from major to lieutenant colonel and,
in a move important for the future, opened contacts and formed a friendship with the commandant of the British Army's Camberley Staff College,
Major-General Henry Wilson—both officers having very clear views on
the likelihood of a war with Germany when the two armies would be in
alliance. In 1911 Foch became a division, and a little later an army corps,

commander. The outbreak of war in 1914 found him in command of the XX Corps stationed in the Lorraine.

Foch was a highly intelligent officer who had earlier published two works on the principles and the conduct of war.[2] The revised 1907 edition of the second included his reflections on the Russo-Japanese War. He did not, however, fully appreciate the major new developments that the Russo-Japanese War had initiated, in particular the defensive capabilities of barbed wire and machine guns, nor, although they were used in Morocco by the equally gifted French commander Hubert Lyautey, the value of aircraft for reconnaissance. Foch had been a strong believer in the strategy of attack in Lorraine and Alsace and was to remain convinced throughout the war that when possible, attack was the best method of defense. In his position as commander, others had not found him an easy general to serve, and he had enemies.

A comparison of temperaments and personalities of Foch and Weygand shows how they complemented each other. Both men were gifted with indefatigable energy and could work under enormous pressure. Foch was a man of action, lively, but he did not always think through his ideas or express them clearly.[3] Weygand was more relaxed and restrained; his mind was at work analyzing and setting ideas and projects against the context of the current situation. He totally understood his chief's mind and could clarify and verify Foch's projects and redact written instructions into clear plans intelligible to subordinates and visitors. In charge of his staff machine, he could provide all the combat and logistics detail administration needed, leaving the grand designs and arguments over moral force and maneuver to Foch. He had a further ability in assessing the suitability of officers for particular command or staff posts, which assessment he could present to Foch free from any favoritism or prejudice. Weygand's ongoing but less evident problem of short temper appeared only when dealing with difficult subordinates.

Foch could see the great intelligence, memory, and administrative ability of his chief of staff. He could draw on his ideas and bounce his own back on Weygand with no weakening of his authority as the commander, and with no fear that his chief of staff had his own agenda, his own ambitions, or his own relationships with subordinate commanders. Weygand was self-effacing and totally loyal; if he was ever the sole architect of any particular plan or operation, he never claimed it. He was courteous and tactful with French and foreign visitors to Foch's headquarters; he was patient and a good listener.

Foch liked Weygand's company. He would often drop into his chief of staff's office first thing in the morning for a discussion over a new idea. At other times he would stride up and down in Weygand's office smoking a pipe, discussing operations, or debate them on motor-car journeys. In return Weygand would shield Foch from the unwelcome ideas or interference of others; Foch did not suffer fools gladly. Throughout the war and its immediate aftermath, Foch was only rarely seen at conferences without Weygand at his side. On their appearances together their relationship was clear and on display: Foch short but stocky in front, Weygand even shorter and slim, a few paces behind. Not the least important of the factors that bound them was that both were unostentatious but very devout Roman Catholics.[4]

Throughout the war Weygand attended Mass on Sundays whenever possible. Both he and Foch believed that in their duties they were serving the Almighty in a war that was morally justified and would eventually end in victory. Foch always referred to Weygand in terms of highest praise: "Weygand, he is a paragon," "Weygand c'est moi"; or when asked a question he would answer, "Ask Weygand, it is the same."[5] In turn Weygand drew the analogy "the Marshal is the locomotive, I am the tender that provides him with coal and water." One of the most remarkable military partnerships in history, it was a two plus two equals five relationship that would last until the end of the war and afterward.

Anglophone readers may find it useful to reflect briefly on the differences in command style between, for example, British and French generals. With one notable exception, Sir William Robertson, who rose from the ranks (helped by his riding skills), British Army generals of the time came from the aristocracy, squirearchy, or upper-middle-class bourgeoisie. They operated within a common class culture. If they differed, however sharply, even if the issue involved replacement or dismissal, their differences were constrained within civilized limits. Arguments could be advanced forcefully; anger, even temper, could be displayed, but never to excess. They might attend different churches, Anglican, Presbyterian, or very rarely Roman Catholic, but religious friction or anticlericalism in any form never appeared. Political interference drew the generals together in opposition. Their approach to any situation was usually practical and phlegmatic even under stress. Showmanship was considered bad form, as years later General Bernard Montgomery was to experience. And above all an enemy army was never fighting on Kent or Sussex ground with destroyed towns, burned houses, dead British compatriots and friends, and facing a dangerous threat to London.

French generalship was different in style, reflecting both the national temperament and the cultural heritages of French history. As a people French men and women are more demonstrative, agitated, and excited in their daily round of activities, on occasion displaying in political affairs an often unrestrained excess on days of street revolutions. The legacy of history for decision makers became for many a tug of war between the Roman law, Roman Catholic, and later Jacobin, centralist authoritarianism, and spirited rejection of that authority when it was obviously unjust or wrong released elements of passion—a clash with Cartesian reasoning that resulted in very mixed attitudes toward authority.[6] When to this mixture was added the second occupation of France in forty-five years—occupation of large areas of the nation's territory by a destructive and oppressive foreign army—the result was passionately held views and explosions of temper in the comportment of the French when they differed with each other or with generals of Allied armies. There were wild gestures, shouting, and slamming of doors. Such behavior made coordination or even cooperation with Allies impossible. General Charles Lanrezac, otherwise a very capable general, could not work with the British Army's commander in chief, Sir John French, and was offensively rude. A classic example is provided by one of Foch's biographers, Liddell Hart, describing a meeting between Joffre and a later British commander in chief, Sir Douglas Haig. Joffre had requested Haig to make an attack in one area; Haig had declined, opting for another. "This infuriated Joffre who simply went for Haig and, as Foch said, was quite brutal. Haig said he was not speaking, as one gentleman to another, and old Joffre said he would have no further dealings with Haig over the matter and that they must work it out with Foch."[7]

Or almost certainly in such cases, Weygand. French history, revolution and postrevolution, with its sharply divided fault line separating views on religion and what should constitute an army, affected generals and generalship throughout Weygand's life with political intrigue and interferences. Generals had to face an enemy army in front but also keep a watch on what political figures and often other generals were conspiring behind their backs. Joffre owed his appointment as commander in chief as much to his reputation as being a good Republican as to his military abilities, and throughout the war left-wing politicians in Paris maintained that the war might provide right-wing generals with a pretext for a military coup.

Foch had not made an auspicious start in the first weeks of the war. Full of offensive spirit, he had allowed his XX Corps to advance too far and, either ignoring an order to pull back or, as he later claimed, having never received it, had suffered a costly reverse at the Battle of Morhange on August 20, 1914. Joffre, however, retained Foch's command (while dismissing a large number of others), actually promoting him to the command of a *détachement* composed of now tired and unattached regiments to be grouped into the new Ninth Army on the Marne, east of Paris. At this moment, the end of August, it seemed that the German advance on Paris was unstoppable, and plans were being made in the capital for the evacuation of the government.

In firm command of the Ninth Army, Foch, who disliked being surrounded by large groups of men, opted for a small select staff of not more than six or seven officers immediately around him. These included Weygand's choice of Captain Pierre-Henry Desticker as head of the 3rd Bureau Operations, where he was to serve for the next four years as a key figure; Lieutenant Boisseau, a future general; a small secretarial staff; a small personal escort; and some twenty-five vehicles. On September 5, at a critical moment during the Battle of the Marne, Foch and Weygand had a brief spat. Foch had retired to bed in a local hotel the previous evening; Weygand, fully dressed, had retired to a caravan nearby. At 4 AM Joffre's order for no further retreats and an attack on the following day arrived. Weygand took the order to Foch, adding a draft order with some apparently complicated administrative arrangements for a later counterattack. Foch rather tersely replied to say the simple order to stop was enough. Weygand responded to the effect that one could halt either intelligently or stupidly, to which an angry Foch retorted that Weygand had not grasped his order, that he was impertinent, should hold his tongue, and write out an order. There followed a few moments of heavy silence after which Foch directed that Weygand should add similar instructions to those which he had prepared earlier. The incident was not mentioned again, and two months later Weygand was made an officer of the Legion of Honor. The spat appears to have been one of those rare outbursts of temper that consolidate a relationship. Both men realized how much they could achieve by working together.

The first Battle of the Marne (September 5–12, 1914) was high drama. By its close, both armies were at the breaking point from exhaustion, so important was the defense or loss of the prize, Paris. Weygand backed all the movements of divisions as directed by Foch with clear orders and effective administration in the defensive, counteroffensive, and pursuit phases of the battle. At one point he flew with one of France's earliest military aviators, Marcel-Georges Brindejonc des Moulinais, to make a personal reconnaissance of the battlefield, at the time a novel achievement for a senior staff officer. The fatigue of the already-exhausted rank and file became so great that desertion posed a serious problem. Among Weygand's duties was the unpleasant one of implementing Joffre's very severe orders for punishment of deserters. On September 9, he was sent forward to corps and division headquarters to finalize plans for counterattack and was given authority by Foch to change the timing of the assault if he thought it necessary. The strain on both men was now considerable. Liddell Hart records the night of September 10 being spent by both on the floor of their town hall headquarters on mattresses, freezing cold, only slightly ameliorated when they were each given one blanket. Weygand later recalled that this was Foch's only entirely sleepless night until November 1918. The battle was eventually won and Châlons recaptured. Foch gave thanks to God with the city's bishop for the victory and full acknowledgment to his chief of staff for his part in securing it. The partnership between the two was now firmly established. Weygand was promoted to full colonel early in the following year.

After a final defensive battle against a German counteroffensive at the end of September, new responsibilities fell upon Foch and Weygand. Joffre, who had a very high regard for Foch, appointed him assistant chief of staff. Faced with the ongoing threat to the French Army's left flank caused by the main strategic thrust of the German Army sweeping through Belgium, Foch was given overall responsibility for coordinating the work of the French, British, and Belgian armies in halting the German drive. Weygand accompanied Foch on a visit to the zone of his new, somewhat ill-defined command. A little earlier Foch had been told of the deaths in action of both his only son and his son-in-law; his relationship with Weygand grew more paternal.

Foch was now faced with serious command problems and difficulties. The terrain, especially near the coast, was low-lying. Deep trench digging was often impossible, and less well dug trenches were muddy and insalubrious. There were two French armies under his authority, the Tenth Army under General Louis Maud'huy, with whom he was quickly able to establish a working relationship, and the Second under General Edouard de Castelnau, who had been his army commander in Lorraine and with whom he had fallen out over the Battle of Morhange (August 20), Castelnau blaming Foch for the defeat. These two armies naturally rated the protection of Paris as their primary role. There was also the British Expeditionary Force (BEF), whose commander, General Sir John French, had not worked well with Joffre and distrusted him. After the retreat from Mons and early spectacular German drive through Belgium, the French felt, and Foch appreciated, that the British must always keep one eye on the Channel ports in case of a French army collapse and the need for an evacuation home. And there was the Belgian army, small and not always well-trained but well-spirited, headed by its king, Albert I, who was desperate to retain a toehold on some small area of Belgian territory, a hope centering upon Ypres. Finally, there was Foch himself—charismatic, inspirational, and brilliant in concepts but neither trained, nor at this period well-suited, to work with others who had different ideas and priorities. Foch had come to realize that, however gallant, mass attacks by infantry could bring heavy casualties and little success. His command at this time reflected the tussle in his mind: the logical analytical part acknowledging reality, his temperamental part seeking opportunities for attack and counterattack, orders for the latter often expressed with vigor, energy, and gesture but not always clearly or fully to subordinates and visitors. To Weygand fell the task of briefing Foch, of developing and clarifying Foch's ideas to Allies, of acting as a sounding board for

Foch to discuss his projects, of helping to make a front deployment plan that satisfied all concerned and inspired French and Allies to fight on tenaciously, and of ensuring that the intelligence operations and logistics staff was on top of the heavy day-to-day volume of work they had been called upon to perform.

For the Belgians Foch was able to provide assurance that Dixmude would be defended (by a gallant force of *fusiliers marins*) and every effort would be made by both the British and the French to hold Ypres. With his previous prewar experience of discussions with the British, Foch was able to repair any damage caused by Joffre and to lay the foundations of an alliance intended to last for the whole war. He made this quite clear to Castelnau, who in theory now issued the orders. The opening of sluice gates and flooding of large areas denied the Allies much room for maneuver, and a plan was developed that provided for Belgian deployment at the coast, with the British in the center and the French armies on the sector's right flank. Two massive German assaults—on the Yser between October 17 and November 1, and around Ypres (known to the British as the First Battle of Ypres) between October 21 and November 12—were halted, but counterattacks ordered by Foch achieved little. Foch attributed this to inadequate artillery and ammunition supplies. But the infantry casualties were heavy.

It is not possible to say in what measure during all this high military drama Foch and Weygand played their respective parts. If, as is very likely, Weygand was alarmed at the loss of life in Foch's counterattack, he kept his counsel. There was no great victory; the front was stabilized, but the Germans remained on the other side of it. It could have been much worse. The success that was achieved was justly credited to Foch, who in turn justly credited Weygand for all his tireless work in support of his command.

In late November and December of 1914, Foch recovered his optimism and ordered an offensive, to be complemented by a further French offensive in Champagne involving the Tenth and Second Armies, the BEF, and the Belgians (now forming the Eighth Army). Every one of the attacks was a failure, costing very heavy casualties and causing a great deal of friction between Joffre and Sir John French. The casualties, together with those of the counterattack at the end of the first Ypres battle, sullied Joffre's and

Foch's reputations, which rival generals and political leaders began to exploit. The consequences for Foch and Weygand that would follow in the New Year were to be serious.

Early in January 1915 Foch was formally appointed as commander of the Northern Group of Armies with authority over the BEF and the Belgians as well as the French Sixth and Tenth Armies. It was a very difficult command. The commanders of the Central Group of Armies, to his right, were Joffre until July and then de Castelnau, who hated Foch. Joffre noted stormy meetings between the two, and Castelnau openly called Foch "the madman of the north." The Belgians were in the last resort, commanded by their king, and happily for Foch Albert was very cooperative. The British were still commanded by French, with his uncertain temperament and distrust of Joffre. Fortunately the arrival of Foch's old friend Wilson on French's staff greatly improved working arrangements. When Haig replaced French in December 1915, a working relationship between Foch and Haig based on mutual respect if not always mutual agreement began; it was to last until 1918.

The ebb and flow details of the bloody battles of 1915 belong to biographies of Joffre, Foch, and Sir John French rather than Weygand, but an overview is necessary for their cumulative effect on Foch, and therefore Weygand, to be understood. Operations began early in the year with limited-scale harassment attacks along the whole Western Front. On Foch's front in Artois the aim was to cause the Germans severe casualties and harass their lines of communication, road and rail. The attacks achieved virtually nothing. The first large-scale French offensive was launched in Champagne in mid-February; it lasted a month and cost 40,000 casualties. On Foch's front Joffre planned for an attack in Artois for early March, but Sir John refused to cooperate, instead launching an attack of his own at Neuve-Chapelle, which proved unsuccessful. There followed the violent German attack that lead to the Second Battle of Ypres, opening on April 22, 1915, with the first use by the Germans of poison gas, which caught all of Foch's command, French, British, Canadian, and French North African troops by surprise. The German attack failed only because they had made no adequate provision to follow up its initial success. On May 9, Joffre mounted a second large-scale attrition attack in Artois, opening with a six-day artillery bombardment. The month-long French and British assault produced only very small territorial gains at enormous loss of life. Failure was attributed to inefficient ammunition, the inability of shrapnel shells to break down barbed wire defenses, and the difficulties of bringing second echelon formations forward sufficiently quickly to exploit the limited local successes.

Both French and British armies increased their strengths during the summer, and in September Joffre launched two massive offensives simultaneously, one in Champagne and one in Artois, with the hope of causing the collapse of the German center and so liberating the German-occupied areas. The Artois attack involved twenty divisions, the Champagne twenty-seven. Despite heroic efforts neither attack achieved more than very limited gains. The explanations offered claimed that one more determined assault would have brought success, and included the fact that the long preliminary artillery bombardment indicated the direction of the attack to the Germans. To these explanations were added the shortage and unsatisfactory manufacture of ammunition, the limited trajectory of the 75mm gun, and the strength of the well-sited and well-prepared German defensive positions, which were often situated on higher ground. The plain, inescapable fact, however, was the mounting total of casualties, which were to prove even greater than those to be suffered by the French at Verdun in the following year—over 1.2 million, of which 350,000 were killed or missing.

For traditionally minded French officers, in particular Foch, these horrifying totals involving fellow countrymen, friends, and sorrowing families were a formidable shock. The struggle in Foch's mind proved ever more difficult to resolve, reason pointing to the casualties but temperament unable to discard entirely the belief that attack was the only way to clear the Germans out of occupied France and Belgium and to achieve victory in the war. For Foch, and therefore also Weygand, the balancing argument became one that superior numbers, the most careful preparation especially with the artillery "creeping" barrages, the rapid arrival of second echelon formations now made possible with the wartime expansion of motor vehicle transport, and a totality of effort without distractions such as the Macedonian campaign or support for Italy together would lead to a victorious attack. Trenches and barbed wire could still be broken and the enemy forced to withdraw.[8]

The overall strain led Foch to outbursts of anger and rage, on occasions falling upon Weygand, who was conveniently to hand usually sixteen hours out of twenty-four each day. An observer of one of these occasions noted Foch returning to Weygand's office very shortly afterward and saying, "You know, Weygand, when I am angry it is not against you but against myself because I have not succeeded sufficiently in making myself understood even though I feel that I am right."[9] Perhaps only the constant activity demands of staff work prevented Weygand from asking for a posting elsewhere; his campaign notes reflect his concern over the ever-increasing casualty lists.

The casualties also increased political criticism and sour observations from other generals, including notably General Maurice Sarrail, who was favored by the political Left but who was dispatched to Macedonia for his intrigues, and also Castelnau. General Philippe Pétain with his meticulously planned artillery-based attacks with modest aims now was also appearing a rival. Damage to Foch's position was limited, but only for one more year.

One positive command- and staff-level consequence of the events of 1915, though, was the greatly improved inter-Allied understanding and cooperation. The two main armies, French and British, learned to work together—how each other's staff procedures operated, what were the personalities of each other's commanders, and that persuasion was more productive than authority. Despite very different habits and attitudes, men in trenches formed a mutual respect for each other's fighting qualities. Weygand's tact, patience, and communication abilities played a valuable part in the development of this mutual respect and comradeship. From this working relationship with the British, Weygand himself developed a respect and liking for his country's ally. Most British officers were happy in this collaboration. There was, however, one exception, the young British liaison officer of 1914, Edward Spears, with whom the French shared an intense mutual dislike, a dislike that was to reappear in May 1940 in even more serious circumstances.

Joffre, with advice from Foch and therefore no doubt Weygand, prepared a new thinking for the next year, 1916. From its nature one may assume that Pétain, with his stress on artillery preparation, may also have had a hand in this new thinking. On the ground, a massive summer offensive on the Somme was to be the centerpiece. For this attack, planned for July 1, 1916, Foch's Northern Army Group would attack together with the BEF, Foch on either side of the river and Haig to the north. The massive German onslaught on Verdun, which began on February 21, forced changes to the plan. The Germans believed that by a sufficiently heavy and prolonged offensive they could destroy the French Army entirely. Foch lost the Tenth Army to the center and was warned that ammunition was running short. Foch continued planning for July, but as the situation at Verdun worsened resources were diverted away from him.

Foch was injured in a motor accident, requiring him to take a period of rest. His enthusiasm for the Somme operation declined as it became clearer that his role on July 1 would primarily be to support the British rather than be a partner with them. Logistic and transport supply problems also appeared. By mid-June the role for Foch's remaining formations had, in effect, become to relieve the German pressure on the French at Verdun and thereby also deter the Germans from taking formations away from Verdun to fight at the Somme. When plans for July 1 were finally prepared, Joffre acceded to the British commander's plans and preferences, which Foch and Weygand believed to be unsound, a view that Foch expressed too openly. When the Somme offensive opened, all that Foch was left with was a small army of seven divisions. In the July fighting Foch's formations fought well, gaining more ground at less than the terrible costs suffered by the British. On July 3, a very heated dispute erupted when Joffre, Haig, and Foch differed over the next moves, the occasion of Joffre's "brutal" outburst noted earlier, but Wilson, Foch, and Weygand soon restored a measure of cooperation. In the months that followed the French Army, better prepared and pursuing its own priorities, made further gains, while the British, to secure their advance, were ill-prepared for the fighting in woods and suffered further heavy casualties. Foch received reinforcements in the form of a new army. Historian Jean Christophe Notin's comments on the whole 1916 Somme campaign well summarize the outcome: the initial strategic object of the battle was a fiasco, but the French acquired objectives during the fighting that obliged the Germans to withdraw divisions. The Homeric battle of Verdun carefully monitored by Weygand's staff provided France with an important and historic victory.[10]

Weygand continued to develop his role as Foch's partner and alternate during the long series of battles, drafting orders and on occasions at Foch's request delivering these in person to subordinate commanders, adding any necessary explanations or soothing friction. Destremau cites an occasion in October after an attack by Foch's Sixth Army had been a failure, incurring Foch's displeasure: the army commander, General Emile Fayolle, wrote, "Foch had again annoyed me, but fortunately I saw Weygand this morning and it is all cleared up."[11] Foch himself was not always in the best of health, at times requiring treatment, but in any period of absence Weygand was deputized.

A journalist visitor to Foch's headquarters, Raymond Recouly, provides an interesting description of the staff. The headquarters were in a villa near Villers-Bretonneux: "General Foch was living in a villa surrounded by a charming park, and he invited us to lunch. His staff-officer shared his table, as well as General Weygand and the liaison of the British General Staff, Colonel Dillon, a typical Irish gentleman, tall, thin and wiry, ruddy of face and apparently quite at home among his French counterparts. There was also a Belgian major and five or six French officers. As usual, Foch's staff was small, but the efficiency of its members more than made up for any shortage." Recouly goes on to describe the general good humor, and the absence of any trace of stiffness or restraint. Even allowing for the fact that no doubt all present would have been told to be on their best behavior, these comments do suggest a happy and efficient headquarters.[12]

On the wider national stage, however, serious issues were emerging, in particular the huge casualties, which in the case of France were now over 200,000 killed, wounded, or missing. There was general dissatisfaction at the progress of the war. Leading political figures blamed Joffre, drawing comparisons with the success of the rising star at Verdun, General Robert Nivelle, in recapturing Fort Douaumont. Other generals who disliked and disagreed with Foch, notably Pétain and Castelnau, expressed misgivings. Only Georges Clemenceau, at the time not a minister, was prepared to support him, though not Joffre. It was not politically possible to remove Joffre entirely from the war effort as that might suggest that the French Army had been defeated. Instead he was appointed as a "technical adviser" to the government with no command of frontline troops. Nivelle was made commander in chief of the armies of the North and Northeast, with Castelnau in command of Foch's Northern Army Group. Accused wrongly by his critics of being unfit, Foch was nevertheless retained by Nivelle for "special missions." The changes all led to furious recriminations between Joffre and Foch over the planning for all present and future operations and the resources allocated for them, but there were no recriminations against other commanders.

For Weygand, in addition to being in the midst of these changes and recriminations, there were two consequences. The first was some intensification of his long-standing dislike of politicians, dating back to the Dreyfus affair. Weygand saw, correctly enough, senior political leaders, some of the political Left, who in his view understood nothing of military matters, interfering in strategy and in the appointment of senior field commanders, and he took exception to their treatment of his chief, Foch. Inquiries from these politicians, obviously hoping for the answer that they did not receive, were made to Weygand about the exact state of Foch's health; Weygand replied firmly that Foch was in excellent health.

The second consequence, with Foch shelved and at the time with no real prospect of returning to battlefield command, was the personal dilemma for Weygand of whether he should leave Foch, and if so where should he go. Foch put the question to Weygand, asking him what he would prefer. Weygand, now a junior brigadier general, replied that he would choose command of an infantry brigade, and Foch directed him to prepare an official application. Infantry was a curious selection for a cavalry officer, though many cavalry officers and regiments had answered the appeals to change from horses to the trenches. Weygand went further. In later writing he describes watching an infantry regiment on the march as the most moving spectacle of the war; in it were to be seen young men barely more than children, older men with jobs and families, all united under fire, the men who carried the heaviest burden in battle.

Foch received from Nivelle a new specific if unexciting instruction. He was told that he was to make a study of a possible German attack on France's eastern border through Switzerland, a threat that had worried Joffre for some time. For this assignment, he was to be allowed a staff, and was instructed not to distance himself too far from General Headquarters. Upon returning from a brief absence, Foch turned to Weygand and told him that he had forwarded Weygand's application, but he still retained a freedom of choice. Weygand's reply was instant: he wished to remain with Foch.[13] On paper this was not a good career move. Weygand would almost certainly have very quickly received command of a division and before long command of a corps. But while honor and sense of duty were no doubt the deciding factor in Weygand's mind, it is also very likely that he may have believed that before long France would need the services of so able and charismatic a leader as Foch in a very senior command. Although it was not Weygand's practice to speak much of his firm religious beliefs, there may also well have been a touch of spiritual conviction that his duty lay with Foch.

After a relatively quiet period of less than six months the Foch/Weygand partnership was again to be called upon in another major crisis, with Foch's chief of staff, little known outside the Northern Group of Armies, now featuring on the international staff. These quiet months, however, gave both men an opportunity to recoup energies.

Foch set up a headquarters at a hotel at Senlis, near Paris, but his own work on plans to meet an invasion mounted from Switzerland was interrupted by a period in command of the Eastern Group of Armies, standing in for Castelnau, who had been sent on a mission to Russia. Activity at the front was limited. The Germans were preparing their withdrawal to the Hindenburg Line and the new French commander in chief, Nivelle, was planning his offensive on the Aisne.

Weygand continued to work on the Swiss frontier attack contingency Plan H. The Swiss government had itself become increasingly concerned about the possibility of such a German attack but saw the appearance of strict neutrality as its priority. In mid-March, however, the chief of staff of the Swiss Army, Colonel Theophile Sprecher von Bernegg, was authorized to open talks with the French.

On April 5, 1917, Weygand arrived in Berne with a staff colonel from army headquarters and a railway expert, the newly appointed general's first single appointment on an international mission. It was agreed that France would intervene in Switzerland only in the case of a major breach of neutrality, and then only with French or British troops. Discussion then focused on the numbers involved, the possible artillery and troop moves, and tactical cooperation. It was also agreed that the two armies could be under French command. In France it was envisaged that this would be an Army Group Switzerland; Foch was thinking in terms of some forty divisions. Following these understandings, Swiss Army officers were sent to learn about the French experience on the Western Front. They soon realized that they were badly out of touch with the warfare of the time.[14] Discussions and negotiations ended with a formal agreement early in 1918.

Other project plans that involved Weygand as much as Foch in the first four months of 1917 included operations in Alsace and in Lorraine and possible support that might be given to Italy—directly if the Germans entered Switzerland or indirectly with artillery or logistic support on the Italian Isonzo Front. In connection with the latter the British Army's Chief of the Imperial General Staff, General Sir William Robertson, took Weygand with him as the French representative on an inspection visit to Italy, a second chance for Weygand to appear in the topmost circles of commanders and to add to his knowledge and experience of inter-Allied politics, foreign generals, and staffs with different agendas and priorities. Foch and Weygand were also briefed on Nivelle's plans for his April offensive, both expressing their misgivings and noting the plans showed no new tactical thinking, but simply a repetition of all that had failed in earlier operations.

Although free from the stress of frontline combat day and night staff work, Weygand became restless. The more he saw of politicians the stronger became his suspicion and dislike of them and their behavior, which he viewed with soldierly disdain. In turn, some political figures began to have reservations about him. He was again considering requesting a field command posting when the whole military scene changed following the disastrous failure of Nivelle's offensive. This had begun on April 16 following a weeklong artillery bombardment. By the 20th, it had ground to a halt after having suffered enormous casualties, including 30,000 dead and 100,000 wounded, and had gained very little ground. Morale of the frontline soldiers fell to a new low and was followed by serious disciplinary unrest beginning in mid-April. There were with riots in some camps, troop trains and railway stations were smashed, troops deserted, and regiments refused to return to the trenches. The troubles lasted until June, but they incapacitated the French Army for much longer.

Nivelle's offensive had been badly planned and fought over ill-suited ground. Details of the assault were known to the Germans through breaches of security. Nivelle's removal from command proved difficult. In what was clearly a grave national crisis General Pétain, despite his known contempt for politicians, was appointed chief of staff of the French Army on April 29 and on May 15 commander in chief, with Foch as chief of staff. Nivelle was finally removed, almost forcibly and amid shouts and abuse, on May 19. Pétain then embarked on the task, his greatest achievement, of restoring discipline and morale in the French Army. Foch's new appointment once more forced a decision upon Weygand, whether again to stay with Foch or take a formation command appointment. He wrote to his wife: "I would have preferred the front line, but you know that I have decided to forget my preference and go wherever I can to be of use to my chief."[15]

Military operations in the second half of 1917 centered, of course, on the British Army's massive "Third Ypres" series of operations. Pétain was able to achieve morale-boosting small successes with his specialty—local, well-prepared assaults that stopped immediately once their local objectives had been secured. The fact remained, though, that both the French Army and the German formations facing it were exhausted. Planning on both sides centered on fresh manpower—for the Germans the many divisions that could be returned from Russia, for the French the arrival of the United States Army. The early months of 1918 were clearly to be the last remaining chance for the Germans to enjoy numerical superiority.

With his appointment as army chief of staff, Foch had been given extra authority, equal to that of the commander in chief, Pétain, with whom until mid-1918 he remained in general agreement. Foch's duties were now at the Allied summit level of decision making, and Weygand's staff skills and personal diplomatic tact became ever more valuable. Differences between Pétain, Foch, and the British prime minister, David Lloyd George, on the one hand and the British generals Haig and Robertson on the other over the prospects of success for the British Flanders offensive, the degree of help to be given to the hard-pressed Italians, and whether the Macedonian campaign should be scaled down required numerous visits and meetings and occupied much of the summer of 1917 summer. Foch believed that Pétain's limited attacks were the best that could be done at the time. Working part of his time with Pétain, Weygand formed a great respect for him, which many years later was to prove of great importance.

Covert intrigues continued, some still against Foch, and Weygand had to spend time and energy discreetly watching Foch's back, sometimes withholding the details from Foch, tact and discretion being the wiser course. Weygand had to pretend to be ignorant of rumored political activities of a questionable nature, and he would abruptly cut short visits with individuals anxious to interest him in some dubious enterprise. These included a coterie seeking to replace Pétain by Joffre, another looking for the replacement of Foch, another general demanding immediate action to counter an enemy attack that he believed imminent (contrary to the assessment of Weygand's intelligence staff), and yet one more, a very senior general asking questions about Foch's temperament, alleging that he was violent. Most curious of all was a statement by Pétain, a notorious womanizer, that he intended to visit Mme. Weygand at her house in Brittany. (His motives appear to have been intrigue rather than amorous.)[16]

One consequence of the different views on Allied strategy was a strengthening of a view that the Allied effort must be better coordinated. The need became urgent after the Italians suffered a very serious defeat at Caporetto in October 1917, leaving the Italian army on the verge of collapse. The British were not yet willing to accept an overall Allied forces commander. Instead, after a meeting of the French and British prime ministers, Paul Painlevé and David Lloyd George, a Supreme War Council (swc) with headquarters was established in Versailles, which included the French, British, and Italian prime ministers with one other senior minister and three permanent military members—Foch, his British friend Wilson, and the Italian General Luigi Cadorna. A little later General Tasker Bliss of the United States Army joined the council. A change of government in France followed in November, Clemenceau, "The Tiger," replacing Painlevé. Clemenceau was also war minister and not disposed to allow Foch, whom he nevertheless admired, to be the spokesman for the French command. Weygand was selected to become the official French representative and was promoted to major general, although Foch continued to attend meetings. It was a curious but effective compromise.

In December 1917 and from January to mid-March 1918 debate revolved around strategy, Lloyd George and Wilson arguing for greater priority for operations against Turkey, opposed strongly by Weygand speaking on behalf of Foch. Pétain argued for a defensive strategy until the arrival of the Americans provided a superiority of numbers. Accepting the need for helping the Italians with artillery, Foch foresaw the coming German offensive and prepared his own Western Front plan. This was submitted to the council by Weygand in January; in essence it provided for attack. If the Germans attacked they should be stopped and a quick counteroffensive launched. If for some reason the Germans did not attack, the Pétain pattern of limited objectives could be continued, with the launching of a major decisive attack to follow. The council agreed with Foch's views, but little detailed planning resulted, one reason being the perennial question of a single Allied generalissimo. Agreement was reached, however, on the need to create strategic reserves, with an executive committee to decide on their deployment. This committee failed to reach agreement, but its importance lay in the selection of Foch as its chairman, a major step toward a future supreme commander.

Weygand's work in this period was to prepare papers for Foch and outline plans for other possible contingencies, such as the prevention of large numbers of prisoners captured on the Russian front and now to be released from prison from rejoining the German and Austrian armies, a contingency prevention project soon abandoned as impossible. There were also issues concerning Allied intervention in southern Russia in support of anti-Bolshevik forces. Weygand was also tasked with providing for much of the training and material help needed by the regiments and formations of the American Army, which on arrival had few machine guns, no artillery, and no aircraft. He also had to deal with internal intrigues, as rival coteries in the SWC, foreseeing the inevitability of a supreme commander, maneuvered in favor of Pétain, Foch, or even Joffre. Weygand continued to maintain discretion, but his posting and his record since 1914 left little doubt about his loyalties and preference.

Before anything concrete had been agreed, the first of a series of massive German offensives opened on March 21, 1918, aiming to cut off the BEF from the French Army on its right flank. The British Fifth Army was broken; the left flank of the rapid German advance once again threatened Paris. A single unified command was now imperative. At a charged emergency conference at Doullens on March 26, Clemenceau directed

Foch to assume the role of coordinator of British and French operations. Weygand was ordered back from the SWC offices to become once again the chief of staff of Foch in a critical battle. A little later, when the military situation was desperate, Foch's position was strengthened when at Beauvais he was given "strategic direction of military operations." The Allies at last had a supreme commander, and with him as his principal assistant was Maxime Weygand.

The radical anticleric Clemenceau was to be the political partner of the devoutly Catholic Foch in the months to follow, each putting his nation first. Initial German successes, particularly in May, led to much criticism and demands for the replacement of Foch by Pétain, who still remained commander of the French Army. Clemenceau respected both men but saw that the temperament of Pétain—lugubrious, strategically cautious, and inclined still to defeatism—could never provide the confidence needed for victory. He made it clear that he himself would resign if Foch were to be replaced. Later he found it necessary to issue a direct order to Pétain to follow Foch's orders. In fairness to Pétain it should be noted that his ideas on defense in depth were very much sounder than those of Foch, saving hundreds of lives.

The German offensives represented a return to the war of mobility, their operational art foreshadowing the blitzkrieg of 1940 with emphasis on speed and mobility. Attacks began with only brief artillery preparations, in order not to reveal the overall plans, and using the new deadly mustard gas. The infantry attacked with the greatest vigor in small groups, wave following wave, providing their opponents with no relief. Aircraft were used in air-to-ground machine gun and bomb strikes. Neither the French nor the British army was prepared for this reinvigorated operational art. The five offensives themselves followed in waves, the first codenamed *Michael* in Picardy, the second *Georgette* opening in Flanders on the Lys on April 9, the third *Blücher*, north of the Aisne on May 27, the fourth, *Gneisenau*, a resumption of *Michael* between Noyon and Montdidier south toward the River Oise on June 9, and the fifth, *Marschenschütz-Reims*, in Champagne on July 15. Foch's strategy throughout these offensives can well be summarized in the well-known frontline trench commander's orders to his officers: "Gentlemen when the barrage lifts . . ." If necessary, German attacks could be recognized to have gained ground; counterattacks need not be immediate, but any opportunity for a limited harassing counterstrike should be taken, and eventually the right moment would come for a great national and Allied counteroffensive.

Much has been written on the tremendous battles following each of the five German offensives; only in the last did the Germans show significant signs of exhaustion. Not an overall history of the campaign, this work will only summarize the major decisions that Foch had to make during each of the five offensives, decisions correctly made, which if they had not been taken could have affected the whole outcome of the war. They represented generalship of the highest order. In the making of these decisions Weygand was at Foch's side for discussion, advice, and staff support, the greatest moments of this remarkable partnership. Foch was now sixty-six; bladder trouble and three and a half years of war had aged him. His vitality and energy remained, but he needed the services of his chief of staff as never before.

Michael, the first of the German General Erich Ludendorff's great offensives, was countered by Foch with one of his most important decisions. The BEF began to fall back toward the Channel; the French fell back to cover Paris. Haig told Weygand that he would need French help near Amiens or he would have to withdraw further toward the coast. Pétain's response was that Paris must be his priority, and he deployed his divisions accordingly. Foch ruled that prevention of a gap opening between the two armies was crucial for the Allied cause, and after ferocious fighting the German advance in both sectors was brought to a halt.

Georgette, Ludendorff's second onslaught, was to have been launched at the same time as *Michael* but became delayed. From April 9 to May 1, it achieved territorial gains and began to pose the same dilemma for Foch. He and Weygand needed all their persuasive powers to restrain Haig from withdrawal to the coast, and Foch personally countermanded Haig's orders to evacuate Dunkirk and destroy its port facilities. To relieve the strain on the BEF Foch ordered Pétain to take over seventy-five miles of the British front and sent him reserve formations to help. Heavy casualties led to Ludendorff's closing down the offensive.

Blücher, the third, late-May onslaught on the Chemin des Dames sector, preempted a local offensive that Foch had hoped to launch in the same area, catching the British and French by surprise and bringing the

Germans once again to the banks of the Marne at Château-Thierry. Paris came under German heavy artillery fire. Foch ordered Pétain to return the divisions sent earlier to assist him in Flanders and overrode his objections and demands for substantial reinforcements, though Haig was ordered to take over a stretch of Pétain's front. *Blücher* was closed down on June 5, but its success, a definite reverse for Foch, led to wide questioning of his ability among politicians, soldiers, and the war-weary general public.

The June 9 offensive southeast of Amiens, *Gneisenau,* was in practice an extension of *Michael's* threat to Paris. It was originally planned to be a follow-up to *Blücher,* but a radio intercept had warned the Allies in advance. The assault gained ground but did not achieve a breakthrough and was ended on June 13.

Marschenschütz-Reims, the last offensive, included a diversionary attack designed to draw troops away from the crucial sector of the Marne front and so enable a final German thrust toward Paris. Foch had a fairly clear idea of the Germans' intentions following very efficient French aerial reconnaissance, but nevertheless the Germans successfully crossed the Marne. Overcautious, Pétain feared again for Paris and ordered that preparations for the use of reserves, earmarked by Foch for an eventual mass counteroffensive, be sent instead to the Marne. A furious Foch countermanded the order, a decision that would prove decisive but would embitter relations with Pétain. The German attack was contained by a vigorous defense, a remarkable combination of French, British, United States, and Italian formations, the French forces including North and West African regiments. The four British divisions that moved hurriedly to the area were led by an Irish general and included Scots and New Zealander units together with a small Australian detachment. By the July 16, German forces and resources were exhausted, and the next day the offensive was halted. Germany's last chance of winning the war was lost.

Inevitably, in these battles so full of national high drama, tensions at political and military levels arose. Pétain and other French leaders were convinced that the British were not providing all the manpower that they could. Pétain was supported by Weygand, who demanded British home defense and older men be sent out to the BEF. Haig and the British asserted that French priorities centered on the defense of Paris with little thought for the Alliance as a whole. There was argument over where and

when reserves should be brought forward, and days and much energy
spent on discussions over how and where the Americans should be deployed. Pétain, Foch, and Haig (faced with desperate shortages of men,
in addition to casualties, some areas now becoming incapacitated by the
first manifestations of Spanish flu) wished to use American divisions
and regiments piecemeal, as and when necessary, to plug gaps in their
own lines. Initially the Americans were reluctantly prepared to accept
the deployment of a regiment or a division for these purposes. As their
numbers grew attitudes changed, but the inexperience of General John S.
Pershing, the American Expeditionary Force commander, led to friction
with Foch. Pershing insisted that American forces must fight under the
command of American officers in their own section of the front. The first
three American divisions, closely followed by a further two, were accordingly sent to Alsace, an area considered at the time to be quiet, to continue
their training.

The threat to Paris posed by the gains made during *Blücher* led to
more heavy criticism of Foch by politicians, Pétain, and other generals,
adding to Foch's burden of command. In July the Belgians created difficulties. The king, reiterating reservations he had made earlier at Doullens, denied Foch authority over Belgian troops. Clemenceau exploded
violently, and all Weygand's tact was needed to prevent an even more
serious rift. During these tumultuous events Foch still commanded,
with a small staff of about twenty men, including Weygand and General
Desticker as artillery adviser, which was known as *la famille Foch* or, on
account of the calm atmosphere at Foch's headquarters, as *la monastère*.

Foch disliked large staffs, but his detractors, notably Pétain, criticized
Foch's small circle. Foch probably believed, in the light of experience,
that the larger the staff the greater would be the number of people seeking
contacts in order to interfere, and that in any case Weygand was so capable
that a large staff would not be necessary. He required a well-heated room,
usually at 80 degrees Fahrenheit, for himself, with Weygand and Desticker
in an adjoining room. The headquarters were first at Sarcut, a village not
far from Beauvais, but they were then moved to Mouchy-le-Châtel and
then again to Bombon, closer to Pétain's headquarters. Foch maintained
a daily routine of work for fifteen hours a day, sleep, an early rise, and a
period for prayer together with well-prepared punctual meals. Important

issues were discussed in his office or on walks with Weygand, who was the only staff officer allowed direct access to him but who, like all the staff, had to work hours governed by operational necessities. Foch accompanied by Weygand would frequently visit (in a Rolls Royce that never broke down) forward headquarters and units during his working day, urging, encouraging, and where necessary remonstrating. Meetings with visitors to Foch's headquarters were never ending. One in late March, when Foch was still in the Beauvais area, included Clemenceau accompanied by Winston Churchill, Weygand's first meeting with the man who would become Britain's prime minister in May 1940. All required staff work preparation; heightened humor and passionate argument were frequent, Foch even becoming angry with his old friend Henry Wilson, who with Lloyd George was attempting to reduce his powers. A visit by Clemenceau, Foch, and Weygand to Lloyd George was necessary to cool tempers. But during and after all the five German onslaughts Foch never lost hope and with Weygand was mentally preparing and planning for the great Allied counteroffensive when the Germans' offensive had run its course. In this context the small size of Foch's staff again came under criticism, now from Clemenceau, the Americans, and the British, and he was obliged to accept change. He enlarged his staff and also his power of control over reserves, both at the expense of Pétain. Weygand now found himself chief of an enormous multinational Allied staff machine, certainly necessary with the arrival of American divisions in large numbers and ongoing sharp debate over their deployment.

With the Germans now no longer capable of offensive action, Foch and his staff began to turn their attention to ending the war in 1918, expressing their own views, in practice often voiced by Weygand, on final offensives and end-of-the-war conditions and arrangements. For Foch his moment had come. Without delay and according to a plan that had been long in preparation, his counteroffensive was launched on July 18. Troops, concealed in woods, emerged with the massive support of artillery, tanks, and aircraft. All were urged on to the attack despite reservations by Pétain. The Germans were first driven out of the salient that *Blücher* had created. Foch's Second Battle of the Marne was the turning point of the Western Front war, representing both his own generalship skills and his unifying of the operations of his French, American, Italian, Belgian, and British soldiers. He was, deservedly, made a Marshal of France, the first since the Franco-Prussian War, with now unchallengeable authority over Pétain. Weygand was promoted to major general.

For the months ahead, ending the war before the miseries of another winter was for Foch the priority. Exhausted, many physically wasted by years of war, and dressed in shabby, faded uniforms, French soldiers stood in sharp contrast to the endless stream of fit, confident American regiments singing on their way to the front. But their arrival also added urgency to the ending of the war. For Foch the victory must be clearly French, with the Allies in support, not a victory of Allies coming to the rescue of France. France must have the lead voice in the postwar settlement to ensure its own future security. Every effort must therefore be made in one last great campaign. Generals who complained that their men were exhausted were met with an abrupt reply that the Germans were even more exhausted.

Much of Foch's time was spent urging on officers and soldiers to efforts that they never believed they could produce. Reservations by Pétain and, at the outset, by Haig were brushed aside. Critics of Foch have claimed that deferring the final offensive to the spring of 1919, with Germany facing internal collapse, would have saved hundreds of casualties. The argument merits mention but is doubtful when viewed in the context of war-weariness, hunger, public health and Spanish flu, and costs to national economies. Weygand was in full support of Foch's strategy; throughout, they remained as one. Attack was to follow attack; the Germans were to be given no respite. Nor was Weygand's staff. On July 23, Foch asked Weygand to prepare a memorandum summarizing the Allies' current superiority in manpower, tanks, and aircraft, and the importance of retaining the initiative, and proposing a program of action. The memorandum, to the surprise of Weygand, was accepted by all the Allied commanders, even after a two-day grumble by Pétain.

Operations then followed the memorandum program. The first big French and British attacks were aimed at clearing the Paris–Amiens railway, which reopened on August 8. Haig was appointed by Foch to command combined British and French armies in the Amiens sector, news personally brought to him by Weygand and giving him much satisfaction. The attacks were very successful, freeing the railway line, the "Black Day of the German Army" unnerving the German commander, Ludendorff. The fighting finished on August 11. On August 17, a French offensive, joined by the British, recaptured ground between the Seine and the Oise. August 26 saw further simultaneous attacks on the Hindenburg Line in the Cambrai area by the British on the north and the French on the south. These attacks forced the Germans out of defenses carefully prepared for the winter. On September 12, American and French troops in twenty-four hours cleared the Germans out of a salient at Saint-Mihiel. At the same time a French attack on the Aisne and a further assault by the British on the Hindenburg Line were slowly making gains.

On September 26, very large French and American forces launched a major assault in the Argonne Forest. The attack achieved only limited success, the French encountering very stiff German resistance and the Americans facing major logistic problems. On September 27 and 29, the British attacked again at Cambrai and St. Quentin respectively, the Belgians attacked along the coast on the 29th, and on the 30th the French attacked on the Aisne. All of these attacks made steady progress at varying rates of advance, Foch continually urging French, British, and Americans alike to make extra efforts.

The last full month of the war opened with a combined British and French attack around Cambrai on October 8. This succeeded in breaking the Hindenburg Line. On the 14th British and Belgian troops liberated Lille. Further south, American and French forces had finally cleared the Argonne by the 10th and were advancing along the Meuse; Laon was liberated on September 13. Before the end of the week the French had finally cleared the Chemin des Dames, the Belgians had cleared the coast, and the British had reached the Scheldt. The final ten days of the war saw a major American offensive on the Meuse that opened on November 1, and reached Sedan on the 6th, with further French and British advances that the Germans, still fighting with determination, were unable to contain.

With the coming of the armistice on November 11, Foch was deprived of his most cherished project, a carefully planned advance into Lorraine.

The stage on which Foch and Weygand were operating was now vast. At the end of September 19, Foch's command on the Western Front comprised 215 divisions, of which 102 were French, 60 British, 39 American, 12 Belgian, 2 Italian, and 2 Portuguese.[17] Staff work for Weygand continued to be as much political military as combat military. It included issues with other French generals, some supported by political figures, other issues with Clemenceau, the prime minister, who had no liking for generals of any stripe, and some more again with the Americans, the British, the Belgians, or the Italians in the all-important coordination of the attacks. In September Clemenceau demanded that Foch request the removal of Pershing for the slow advance, a request that Foch refused. Later, on October 1, when Foch requested some of Pershing's divisions be placed under French command, Weygand had to take the full blast of Pershing's fury. More disputes arose among the Allies over the conditions that should be imposed by the armistice and continued in the days and weeks afterward.

The control exercised by Foch's headquarters in the last month of the war was extended to include wide powers over the railway and rear areas. Officers engaged in debates and plans for the best use of the tanks available at the time and whether the greatly improved aircraft becoming available should be used for strategic bombing in Germany or in support of frontline operations, and handled the requests by the Italians for more help with equipment and troops. One of the angriest confrontations occurred as late as October 24 over Haig's request that one of his armies that had been placed under Belgian and French command be returned to him. Foch eventually gave way. An ongoing difficulty was Clemenceau's intense dislike of Pershing and his argument that the Americans were persistently dragging their feet. With all these issues swirling around him, Weygand had also twice to engineer Foch's moving his headquarters to be nearer the front.

In late October, with both Foch and Weygand tense but exhausted, there appears the second occasion when Foch was angry with Weygand. Pétain advocated maintaining an advance that could have led to entry into Lorraine, which Weygand supported. Foch believed this could not be considered for at least three weeks and snapped at Weygand, calling him "a rash gambling cavalry officer of no culture." It was an explosion like that in 1914 that had no lasting effects whatever.[18]

At the end of September, sharp political differences over the ending of the war arose, when Clemenceau asked Foch's for his views. Foch saw

conditions for a ceasefire to be essentially a military matter, politicians being incapable of understanding the military issues. Foch felt that civilian
leaders should be kept informed but should not be involved until a later,
peace-treaty-making stage had arrived. Weygand, whose already strong
dislike of politicians was not diminished by the controversies developing
later in October, entirely agreed with him; predictably Clemenceau did
not. Clemenceau was now beginning to talk of a Weygand influence on
Foch as something sinister, probably a self-excuse for his own inability to
control the Marshal.

Undeterred, Foch prepared his terms, and at a meeting of commanders
and staff on October 25, he set these out. They involved the immediate surrender of 5,000 guns, 30,000 machine guns, 150 submarines, 5,000 railway
locomotives, and 150,000 war zones with the evacuation by the Germans
from Alsace, Lorraine, Luxembourg, and Belgium. France was to have
immediately at least three large bridgeheads across the Rhine at Cologne,
Coblenz, and Mainz, with later a fourth near Strasbourg; Germany was to
evacuate all troops from the left bank of the river. Further the Germans
were to accept responsibility for the war and agree to pay reparations.
The Royal Navy's blockade, which was inflicting severe hardship on the
German civilian population, was to be maintained until the signing of a
peace treaty. Pétain and Pershing supported the terms but favored conditions even more severe. Foch's rejoinder was that the Germans would
reject harsher terms and might lead to more fighting, with perhaps an
additional 50–100,000 dead. Haig thought Foch's terms were too severe
for the Germans to accept. Clemenceau with the support of President
Woodrow Wilson, whose "Fourteen Points" Foch had completely ignored,
opposed any purely military ceasefire, insisting that civilian political leaders be involved.

The Germans requested a meeting on November 5 in the belief that
terms for an armistice could be discussed. Foch refused the meeting, and
arrangements were made for it to take place on November 9 at Réthondes
in the Compiègne Forest, where access could be controlled and politicians
kept uninformed. At the meeting in the famous railway carriage Foch
read out the terms. The civilians on the German team asked for easier
conditions, but Foch refused any negotiation and simply gave the German

delegation seventy-two hours to decide. With concession on only a few minor details they reluctantly accepted Foch's terms early in the morning on the 11th, with fighting to cease at 11 A M. The "War to End Wars" was over.

Weygand was present with Foch throughout these days and hours, making sure that Clemenceau and any other politicians were kept out. He could emerge from the war with enormous credit and was held in the highest regard nationally as one of the architects of the victory. He now had influence, if not much actual real power, on many government policies. But he also now had enemies. His critics were for the moment muted, but were soon to reappear, claiming that Weygand had been nothing more than Foch's clerk or shadow and that as a general he had never commanded a formation in battle. Clemenceau personally insulted him, sneering at his yellowish skin color.[19] For the anticlerical political leaders, he remained an anti-Dreyfusard, a practicing devout Roman Catholic, and together with Foch he was portrayed, totally unjustly, as being a danger to the Republic, the anticlerical government of France still living in a paranoia of fear of being ousted by a coup of Catholic, clerical monarchists. The passions aroused by the Dreyfus affair sharpened this paranoia. It was to recur in the 1930s. With none of the direct life and death terms and responsibility of command, and with the Belgians as an ally, though, no suggestion appears that the question of his parentage troubled his mind in these years.

The 11th hour of November 11, 1918, was to be the greatest hour in his life and is described with much literary style in his *Le 11 novembre*.[20] Fortune had smiled upon Weygand, but it was not to do so for much longer.

3

⇒+ ⇒+ ⇒+

VERSAILLES, WARSAW, SYRIA
1919–24

Accompanying Foch in November and December 1918, Weygand visited the devastated areas of France that had been occupied by the Germans. He saw wanton German destruction of towns, villages, and farms and talked to surviving inhabitants about the suffering that they had endured. The impressions that he formed were strong and to be recalled in the 1930s: this must never be allowed to happen again, and his country, France, must play the lead role in ensuring that it did not. The impressions were to last his life, especially in May 1940. In these views he followed Foch, who saw French security as the prime issue in the peacemaking. This belief was only strengthened by the events in Germany in late 1918 and early 1919: the German army's triumphal march through Berlin on December 19, the salute taken by the chancellor, Friedrich Ebert, and the rhetoric of the army returning unbeaten from the field of battle, soon to be extended to that of *Dolchstoss,* a stab in the back by politicians. Further, following the Russian Revolution, it seemed clear that France would not expect any massive support on an eastern frontier, while Austria would join Germany.

Foch passionately believed that security, *sûreté,* could be gained only by the Napoleonic dream of the Rhine as the French frontier, creating a buffer zone against this growing strategic imbalance. He unwisely encouraged talk of the Catholic area on the left bank of the Rhine as not being truly German and supported French generals, notably including Fayolle and Charles Mangin in the army of occupation, who tried to sponsor Catholic separatist groups. As a Catholic, Weygand may have been sympathetic to this project; he was certainly later accused of being so. Such talk was silenced very firmly by Clemenceau. Foch argued that politicians had no understanding of the realities of war or military issues and were betraying vital French interests by not supporting a border at the Rhine; that the League of Nations would prove useless; and that agreements promising military support from Britain and the United States were no sure guarantee of help. In arguing these views he met increasing opposition from President Wilson and Prime Minister Lloyd George, Clemenceau, and Vittorio Orlando, whom Weygand described in his diary as "the four old men." They argued that on political and military grounds the separation of the Rhineland and formation of a French client Rhenish state would result in the loss of British support and lead to the kind of destabilizing resentment seen in Alsace Lorraine. In the early stages of the peace process Foch was invited by the Council of Four to appear at meetings where security was being discussed; later, Clemenceau sought to curtail expressions of opinion by Foch. When the national delegations for the Versailles Conference were being nominated, each was to name five members. Foch was attached to the French delegation as a sixth member, but he was given no official voice, a calculated snub from Clemenceau.[1]

Foch and Clemenceau's disagreements continued in exceedingly acrimonious controversy. The Rhineland issue was the openly contested issue; others included the size of a German army and the length of the period of occupation. Behind these disputes lay, once again, the issue of soldiers versus politicians and the post-Revolution and Dreyfus affair fault-line divisions in French national life. Although still enjoying huge popularity in France, Foch was an anti-Dreyfusard and an "establishment" military figure, now being criticized not only by politicians but also by a new generation of frustrated younger officers. For Wilson and Clemenceau, supported by Lloyd George, Foch was speaking out of turn, but in view of his prestige and popularity was very difficult to attack and criticize openly. Attacks again fell upon Weygand, portrayed as Foch's evil genius. Wilson demanded his removal. Lloyd George noted how at meetings Weygand would whisper in Foch's ear—in fact, probably only to calm him down, as Foch never took kindly to anyone telling him what to do. A succession of bitter clashes with Clemenceau worsened, Foch now openly insubordinate and suspected of planning a right-wing government or even a coup.[2]

Weygand followed Foch's arguments and fully supported them, as much by his own belief in them as by his devoted loyalty to the Marshal. He remained as Foch's chief of staff until Foch's resignation, working amid the complex international negotiations and comings and goings with the skills and diplomacy that he had acquired in the war years. On occasion when he thought the company was in accord with his views, he would let slip a rash remark that later became known.[3] He figured, as always, immediately behind Foch in victory parades in London and Paris, particularly enjoying the warm welcome he received in London.[4] Despite his opposition to British policy, which he saw as aiming to return Britain to the leadership of Europe, his liking for Britain and the British grew. Later, in 1920, he was to take a close interest in the project of André Maginot for the burial of an Unknown Soldier under the Arc de Triomphe in Paris.

Personal criticism of him, however, began to mount. President Wilson now claimed that Weygand was using Foch to further his own personal political aims and that in no circumstances whatever would American soldiers serve under the command of Weygand. All this bickering was to further confirm Weygand in his disdain for politicians and helps to explain some of his views and actions in the turbulent France of the 1930s. Foch refused to be present at the signing of the Versailles Treaty on June 28, 1919, claiming prophetically that the treaty would not secure peace but only an armistice for twenty years.

Only a few days after the Versailles Treaty was signed, a new and serious military problem opened in Eastern Europe. Following the end of the eighteenth-century partitions of Poland and the proposed formation of a revived Polish sovereign state, the new nation under the dynamic leadership of Józef Piłsudski had embarked on an unwise military incursion into Ukraine in support of Ukrainian nationalists, with a view to a future anti-Russian alliance. Polish troops entered Kiev on April 7, 1920, but were met with a mixed reception.[5] The Communist government in Moscow had by an early decree of the Council of People's Commissars proclaimed its authority over all the lands and territories of the former Russian Empire (later amended to exclude Finland). Vladimir Lenin accordingly ordered the newly formed Red Army under the very able General Mikhail Tukhachevsky to clear the Poles out of the Ukraine and to enter Poland, hoping that such acts would inspire communist revolutions in Poland and Germany. As the Red Army swept four hundred miles into Poland, a crisis developed for France, which had hoped to form alliances with the new nations emerging on Germany's eastern frontiers. It seemed that the Red Army could not be stopped, its forward units appearing in the outskirts of Warsaw by early August.

British prime minister Lloyd George urged that Marshal Foch be sent to try to coordinate an effective opposition. Both Foch and the French government were reluctant. Could the reputation of France's foremost soldier, a Marshal of France, and the prestige of the French Army be so put at risk?[6] It was decided instead to send Weygand, Foch remarking that his chief of staff would certainly do what he would do. As part of the French aims for postwar Europe, there were already some 150 French officers at work in Poland under General Paul Henrys, among them Captain Charles de Gaulle, helping to form the new Polish Army. In addition to the Red Army threat, Henrys had a number of local problems within Poland, not the least of them being that the Polish government was expected to pay for the French officers at a rate some ten times that of a Polish officer of the same rank. Henrys did not take kindly to the arrival of Weygand, technically his junior. Weygand's first task on his arrival on July 24 was to fashion a smooth working relationship with Henrys. Henrys would remain in charge of the unsatisfactory and pleasure-seeking officers in the training mission, leaving Weygand free to advise the Polish field command.[7]

Both the armies in this small but very important war, a decisive one in that it was to stop Moscow's grand plans for European revolution, had been very hurriedly put together.[8] The Poles suffered from the bitter rivalries and personal jealousies arising from the very different backgrounds and training of commanders whose pre-1918 experience had been with three different armies, German, Austrian, and Russian. Each commander wanted the laurels of a victory over the Bolsheviks for himself, and one or two were prepared to see others fail. Yet each had in common the Polish fear and dislike of Russia and the perception of war more in terms of gallant charges than of logistics, an attitude from which the feisty, proud, and often suspicious Piłsudski was far from free. He had secured the title of Marshal for himself and made it clear that he was to make the major decisions. Weygand found the commander of the Polish Fifth Army on the southern sector of the front, General Władysław Sikorski, easier to work with, and the friendship so formed was to be revived in 1940 when Sikorski was head of the Polish government in exile. Fighting reached its most intensive period during August 12–14, 1920. Thereafter Polish flank counteroffensives began to force the overstretched Tukhachevsky and his cavalry counterpart Semyon Budyonny into an orderly but decisive retreat, with many soldiers deserting on the way.

For Weygand the war was more than one of simple help for an ally. It was a war of a Catholic people against an army of an atheist, materialist creed. There was also a family connection for Weygand: his wife's mother had been Polish. He enjoyed the admiration of the Polish aristocracy, especially the beautiful ladies, and developed a very high regard for the ordinary Polish soldier. It was work for which he was ideally suited and in which he could see results. He turned down a field command appointment and also a formal offer from Piłsudski to become assistant chief of staff—to Piłsudski's annoyance. He saw his role as a counselor and adviser, bringing together and coordinating the projects of the different Polish generals, in at least one case apparently suggesting to some that written communications and plans were less likely to lead to misunderstandings than loose verbal agreements.[9] His advice was always firm, precise, tactful, and loyal. As important as material detail was confidence building. Poland was a fledgling nation, and the advice of a famous French officer was of great psychological significance.[10] Few senior Poles had any real expertise of logistic support, certainly nothing approaching Weygand's extensive experience. And with his knowledge of fighting on the Western Front during the World War, Weygand was able to advise on the frontline defense systems, making sure that trenches were dug and wired around Warsaw. His daily routine, beginning with a situation briefing from his several liaison officers, often included visits to give technical advice and, with other senior Poles, attendance at Mass.

A much smaller British political and military mission was also in place and cooperated fully with Weygand. On the political side, the mission's chief was Lord d'Abernon, and the senior soldier Major General Adrian Carton de Wiart. The British military attaché in Warsaw, Lieutenant Colonel Emilius Clayton (the author's father), who had served with the French Army throughout the Macedonian campaign and spoke French,

German, and Russian, worked closely with Weygand in bringing Polish commanders together.

The honors of victory belong to Piłsudski. Weygand was one of the first to acknowledge this, though initially and for his own political reasons Piłsudski continued to falsely accuse Weygand of claiming the credit. Weygand had played a key role in the battle, a role that sometime later, after feelings had cooled, Piłsudski acknowledged. It is more than doubtful whether Piłsudski would have secured his victory without the staff work of Weygand's team. Much later, in 1935, Weygand wrote that the Polish staff plans for the battle were not originated by him, yet without his experience and support advice the outcome would certainly have been unfortunate.[11] With his usual tact and modesty Weygand made no personal operational claims and, while greatly respected, was seen as a rather cold personality by many Polish officers. Weygand drank little, if at all, during the conflict; the same could not be said of the Polish officers.

And Weygand was once again to find himself the center of political controversy, both in Poland and in France. In Poland he was feted by the aristocracy and gentry, most strict Catholics and anxious to prevent Piłsudski from becoming all powerful as his pre-1918 politics had been socialist. On his arrival at the Gare de l'Est in Paris, Weygand was given a tumultuous welcome by a very large crowd, among them many Catholics and followers of the political right more concerned with political point making and celebrating a victory over Marxists than with the success of a French general. He was promoted to be a *général corps d'armée* (lieutenant general) and within the Legion of Honor advanced to the rank of commander, but he also acquired a new notoriety for the political Left as a Catholic general helping a Catholic army. Shortly after his return and a brief visit to Foch, extreme right-wing politicians fearing the growth of the political Left began speaking of Weygand as a possible leader of a coup. While Weygand had much sympathy with moderate right-wing views, he remained an officer loyal to the Republic. With respect to Poland his own views had become realistic. He liked and admired the Poles, but a medium-sized nation sandwiched by Germany on one side and Russia on the other had limitations as an effective and reliable ally for France. In turn, unfortunately, Piłsudski retained a lasting dislike of Weygand.

Weygand returned to his duties with the Council of the Allies, now supervising treaty implementations with Germany and the difficulties arising from the Turkish rejection of the Treaty of Sèvres and its military revival. He had to spend time in the agreeable Swiss city of Lausanne, where a new treaty was eventually drafted. He found time to attend the funeral of his First World War friend Field Marshal Sir Henry Wilson, murdered by the Irish Republican Army in June 1922.

In 1923, following Germany's deliberate refusal to meet reparation payments, the French Army was ordered to enter the Ruhr, and a project for a new High Commission for the Ruhr was planned. The project was supported by the Parisian press, which called for Weygand to be high commissioner, but behind it also lay the ambitions of other generals senior to Weygand. France already had a general officer in command of the French Army of the Rhine, and General Jean Degoutte and Weygand discussed the proposal with him. Degoutte pointed out that it was desirable that he, as the general commanding, retain the powers of law and order. The project proved to be unworkable, and it was accordingly abandoned, thus sparing Weygand from the jealousies that would otherwise have risen. Weygand also wisely turned down the offer of the appointment as Henrys's successor in Warsaw.

In April 1923 the center right Poincaré government appointed Weygand to be French high commissioner in Syria and Lebanon, areas that had been mandated to France by the League of Nations in 1920. Weygand had never been to Syria and knew nothing about the region, but there for the first time he was to be in command, not a chief of staff. He replaced General Henri Gouraud, who had lost an arm in 1915 in the Dardanelles. He had been injured in an insurgent ambush in Syria and was worn out. An additional reason for his replacement was that Gouraud was a strict Catholic. It appears that the difficulties and cost of the operations in Syria and the need for a senior and prestigious figure such as Weygand, although also a known devout *pratiquant,* were not the only reasons for this apparently illogical appointment. With an eye to the future, the minister for war and pensions, André Maginot, wished to clear Weygand of a reputation of being Foch's protégé.[12]

France had had an interest in Syria for a long time, arising in particular from French protection for the Roman Catholic Maronite community in

Lebanon. At the end of the First World War, a small French detachment had been included in General Sir Edmund Allenby's army that ejected the Ottoman Turks from both territories, and a dubiously binding official wartime agreement on their future had envisaged both territories passing to France.[13] French ambitions had included possession of an "outer ring" of Cilicia in southern Anatolia and Mosul. In Iraq, Turkish national revival had led to the ejection of the French military from Turkey and the British had secured Mosul for Iraq, leaving the French the more determined to hold on to the "inner ring" in Syria and Lebanon. Syria was seen as a hub area for France and a counterweight to the large British presence in the area. Gouraud had conducted a series of severe "pacification" operations and had also summarily removed the Hashemite Prince Faisal, who had been proclaimed king of Syria by a national congress in April 1920. Gouraud then reorganized the territorial borders in the region, giving a substantial area occupied by Sunni and by Shia Melkites and Druze peoples to a separate Lebanon, one greatly enlarged from the former protected Ottoman Maronite Sanjak. By the time of Weygand's arrival on May 9, 1923, the uncoordinated primary resistance of the different Syrian communities had been finally brought under control, with the exception of Turkish-supported Kurds in the extreme northeast.

Gouraud's style had been crudely kinetic; Weygand's style was to be modest, free of arrogance, and conciliatory. He was prepared to listen and to appreciate local conditions and community views. While the two territories still remained in need of gendarmerie and policing by riding camel companies, the only military operation that had to be undertaken was the ending of the Kurdish revolt. Two months after Weygand's arrival a small French military column was massacred, and the heads of three French officers were put on display in a local butcher's shop in a town on the Turkish border.

Weygand did face the usual problem encountered by any senior French officer—political intrigues, some local, based on ethnic, masonic, and religious factions scheming for position or protection of their privileges. There was also some intrigue back in Paris, where almost from the start critics opposed the choice of another Catholic general. In respect of the local rivalries Weygand remained firm. Leaders of earlier and current uprisings were tried quickly by local tribunals and sentenced, some to death, but in other disputes Weygand remained strictly impartial. Troop numbers and military costs were greatly reduced, responsibilities being handed over to local gendarmeries. A number of notably able officials were appointed to the French administration, and Weygand personally interested himself in the development of the two territories' infrastructure, transport, and posts in the economy, in particular exports of cotton and silk. The school system was reformed and a modern university opened in Damascus. Weygand's brief period in office also saw two constitutional reforms. The first was the restructuring of the Syrian administration to one based on the two largest cities, Damascus and Aleppo, with a special administration for the Alawites. The second reform, instituted shortly before his departure, was the joining of the two big regions into a Syrian state to complement the state being formed for Lebanon.

Weygand was surrounded by advisers who counseled him to distrust the British, who they alleged, with very little if any justification, were seeking to oust the French from Syria. They pointed to the greater freedom, flag independence, and League of Nations membership being given to Iraq as evidence of an indirect move by the British to extend their authority. The real difference, however, lay in the contrasting cultural heritages of the two nations. The British common law tradition accepted that local decisions were to be made by the freely expressed choice of local people, while the French centralist Roman law approach aimed at assimilation, the approach behind Weygand's reforms.

Both Weygand and his wife enjoyed life in Beirut. Weygand's daily routine would start with an early morning ride with his personal staff officer, Roger Gasser, and circumstances permitting, an early retirement in the evening. Renée Weygand entertained people from all communities, enjoying the exotic and varied nature and dress. Society enjoyed the change from prewar formality; a measure of *affaires* and gossip was permitted provided it remained within bounds and was not a distraction from duty or a violation of the local conventions of the time. One member of the high commissioner's entourage who engaged in homosexual liaisons was however returned immediately to France.[14]

The May 1924 election victory of the left-wing Cartel des Gauches coalition in France meant the end of Weygand's time in the Levant. Intrigue and false rumors led to his recall by Prime Minister Edouard Herriot early in December. He left Syria and Lebanon with law and order established and the foundations for development well laid. His departure was greatly regretted, even by nationalists opposed to French rule. His successor, General Sarrail, the favorite of the political left, was by his ineptitude and authoritarian arrogance to bring about the catastrophe of the national uprising known as the Druze Rebellion within seven months of his arrival in January 1925. French colonial rule in Syria and Lebanon was very seriously flawed, but Weygand's eighteen months was perhaps its redeeming feature.

Weygand returned to France embittered, resenting his recall, which he saw as the work of political intrigue and jealous military rivals, some by anti-Catholic elements or Freemasons. His bitterness was soon sharpened by Sarrail's actions, which included the artillery bombardment of Damascus, for which he was peremptorily recalled by Paris. For his own work in Syria Weygand was awarded France's highest decoration, the Grand Cross of the Legion of Honor, and promoted to full general. This promotion was not always well received by other generals of lower rank who had commanded formations in the trenches of the Western Front. Weygand was again lauded by the political right to the anxiety of the extreme-left militants, but for Weygand himself there was anxiety about his own personal safety amid rumors of a planned assassination.

4

☰ ☰ ☰

DEFENSE POLICY IN
A FRACTURED FRANCE
1925–39

In the years 1925 to 1939, the bulk of the interwar years, Weygand's life fell into three phases. The first was from 1925 to the end of his tenure as director at the Centre des Hautes Etudes Militaires (CHEM), the second from 1930 to 1935 when he held senior military staff and policy appointments, and the third from 1935 to 1939 when he was technically retired but still possessed very great influence. The whole period was one of both ever-sharpening political and social division, which was worsened in the 1930s by the Great Depression and within the military by the onset and spread of what Marshal Alphonse Juin was to describe, after the end of the Second World War, as a military "sclerosis." The immediate cause of the former lay deep in post-Revolution France. The causes of the second were the loss of so many of the army's sharpest intellects in the trenches, financial stringency, divisive and deep-seated disputes, and, in the 1920s, overconfidence and errors of judgment.

As early as 1925 the change in the political climate following the victory of the Cartel des Gauches in the 1924 general election was clear. Politics was to be about a Franco-German rapprochement, multilateral disarmament, and, in the face of France's postwar economic situation, what savings could be made by reductions in defense expenditure. With the defeat of Germany and the disarmament treaty conditions imposed on Berlin, a future war seemed out of the question, at least for a number of years. In France a communist party had appeared that was sharply antimilitary. Within the military, many commanders, notably Pétain, who was now a Marshal, believed that the real foundation on which victory had been secured was the heroic infantryman. While tanks and aircraft had been useful in the last months of the war, they should not be allowed to take attention away from infantry in well-prepared defense positions. Tanks were seen only as close support firepower, not as the spearhead of a breakthrough. Further, armor and aircraft were exceedingly expensive and would necessitate a professional army rather than one based on conscripts, with attendant political danger. Accordingly in the 1920s, the army's chief of staff, Eugène Debeney, took care to promote and post only officers who would preserve a virtual throwback to a 1914-style army, with bands, parades, and ceremonies much on display. Officers who disagreed suffered in their careers, and among them was the then Major de Gaulle; a number of the most intelligent left in despair. For those who served on, regiments were kept short of necessary equipment with little new provided. Barrack buildings, even military colleges, decayed from neglect, and pay remained at a third of that of a British officer of comparable rank. For many the army was now parasitic. Men and women of all classes, not only the lower-income, gave a man in uniform a hostile stare, and no serving soldier of any rank was allowed to vote. The political Left, in particular the newly formed Communist Party, led a major demonstration and leaflet campaign against the French Army's fighting against Abd el-Krim's Rif uprising in Morocco; two metropolitan conscript infantry regiments ordered to Morocco had marched out of their Paris suburb barracks shouting and singing pro-Rif slogans.

The future for a high-profile general, returning home with laurels gained in Poland and Syria, was a problem for the Paris government. Weygand could not be offered mere command of a military region; as a full general he would have likely refused the offer in any case. Marshal Lyautey suggested that Weygand be offered command in Morocco, where France was fighting the Rif uprising, but because of the political danger should Weygand add a third victory to his record, that idea was rejected. In any case Weygand was a Catholic. Nor could he be returned to Syria, though many requested it, as that would mean loss of face for the government. Command in Germany was out of the question in view of his past association with Foch and the Marshal's separatist views at this time of rapprochement. Finally, an honorable sideways posting was found for him as the director of CHEM, the "School of Marshals." He had earlier been made a member of the Conseil Supérieur de la Guerre (CSG), the nation's supreme defense policy body, and his retirement age had been extended from sixty-two to sixty-five, which age he would reach in 1932.[1]

After the 1924 election the French Army was totally subordinated to the doctrine and policies of the Cartel des Gauches political leaders, Herriot, Briand, and in particular Painlevé in partnership with Pétain. Military colleges, CHEM, the Ecole de Guerre, and Saint-Cyr were expected to conform their teaching and to aim for world peace through the League of Nations, disarmament, and antimilitarism. The climate was one of conformity: do not cause upset by the airing of modern or reformist military theories. If anyone was rash enough to do so, his career prospects would suffer severely. The most attractive postings went to the graduates who could be relied upon not to cause trouble. Weygand, however, had written an article in 1921 in a cavalry journal in which he foresaw armored divisions composed of fast tanks and self-propelled artillery and supported by aircraft strikes. At CHEM he invited a colonel to develop these ideas. The debate that followed left him with a clear realization of the need to keep up with all possible developments in armored and mechanized warfare, but the official view remained one of caution against imaginations perceived as overheated. Weygand could go no further, and all efforts to reinvigorate the command with any offensive spirit faded. Although shaken by the writings of a contemporary German general who claimed that the French Army was good at congratulating itself on past deeds but lacked the moral courage to modernize and the courage necessary for success, Weygand kept his counsel. His teaching style was formal, but in talking with students, *stagiaires,* he was always charming; even outbursts of temper would be followed by a *coup de charme.*[2]

His position in the CSG was delicate. He was a new and junior member in company with marshals and senior generals who had commanded large formations in the war but were now aging and seeking rest upon their laurels. Except for Hubert Lyautey, a cavalryman who attended rarely, other members were all infantry or artillery. Weygand at the time did not see any need for sharp controversy, but he put forward the case for armor with moderation and made sure his views were fully set out in CHEM publications. Two particular staff policy decisions merit mention here. In April 1925 Foch requested and Weygand supported a proposal that a permanently ready intervention force of six cavalry divisions be prepared, a decision approved in October 1926 but never fully implemented. The second decision, that tanks should be included in infantry division formations rather than any specific armored formation, was to prove highly unfortunate. Doubts still remained over the speed and endurance of tanks.

Other major decisions made by the governments of Herriot, Painlevé, and Briand in the late 1920s included a December 1927 plan to demarcate the frontier areas to be reserved for future fortification building, and two March 1928 decisions, one to reduce overall numbers followed by another to reduce the length of compulsory national service for conscripts from eighteen to twelve months, the conscripts' main role to be the training of a civilian reserve force with only a small regular contingent for the frontier defense. Finally came the autumn 1929 voting of credits for the start of the building of what was to become the Maginot Line. Weygand was particularly angry over the shortening of the draft period, already unsatisfied with regular soldiers having to spend more of their time in the endless turnover of basic training rather than training for war as a unit. He also feared the change was the first step towards the replacement of a professional army by civilians in uniform acting as a purely defensive national guard, a goal long sought by the Left. Certainly these measures all marked the triumph of the ministers and generals who favored a defensive strategy.

For Weygand himself the CHEM years were a respite from ten years of hyperactivity, with a more outgoing social life and a large circle of friends and interests. Renée's health had suffered, and hospitality at home had been reduced. He bought a small manor house at Morlaix in Brittany, near one owned by Foch. In Paris Weygand took part in literary, scientific, and artistic circle meetings and discussions, and when time permitted he visited and commented upon places of architectural beauty, including on one occasion Ispahan in Iran. He dressed simply rather than in clothing proclaiming that he was a general in civilian clothes. When in the country walking, even gardening, his clothes were in order. He enjoyed intelligent debate, especially with women, and wrote two books, a biography of Foch and another of the great seventeenth-century French general Turenne, both men with a combination of battlefield skills, ability to lead armies of men from several lands, and Catholic beliefs that obviously appealed to their biographer.[3]

In this period Weygand kept himself fit. His long working days began with riding, in uniform, always smartly turned out and expecting no less from others. He ate and drank moderately so as to retain a trim figure and clear eye. He was devoted to his sons. When the younger son, Jacques, on passing out of Saint-Cyr, opted for the Foreign Legion's elite cavalry regiment, Weygand appears to have been momentarily disturbed. Learning that his son might receive jibes about foreign ancestry, he refused to speak to him for three days. His fears were to prove groundless. To his elder son, Edouard, Weygand once remarked that in November 1918 he would have entered a monastery had it not been for his family. On the few occasions he appeared at a public ceremony, crowd members of the political Right cheered and applauded, while those from the Left booed or sneered. Some still suspected him of political ambitions, even a coup, conspiracy theories of the time to be brought out again in 1940.

In the last two and a half years of the decade, the question was raised about who would succeed General Debeney as chief of the General Staff and later possibly become commander in chief of the army in time of war. Foch, before his death in 1929, had made clear his views—it should be Weygand. The political Left, led by Painlevé, the war minister, wanted General Maurin, a man of sound Republican views but of no particular distinction. Weygand, who viewed his chances with mixed feelings and was not expecting to win, was taken by surprise when Pétain, at the time in the more important post of vice president of the CSG (the president was Painlevé), declared that Debeney's successor in 1930 must be Weygand. At first sight this seemed logical; CHEM after all was the school for the most senior officers. But the addition of support by Pétain was remarkable in view of all the frictions of the past. Pétain accepted that there had been sharp differences over the years, but affirmed that Weygand was the most intelligent and the hardest worker of the time. Pétain further proposed that in 1932, when he himself planned to retire, Weygand should also inherit Pétain's military post as inspector general, which would automatically make him the commander in chief in the event of war. Pétain was much criticized for this selection, the unkind attributing it to age and indifference, but Pétain's decision was more likely based on how threatening events in Germany were becoming. In November 1929 the Briand government fell and the new right-wing government was headed by André Tardieu, who had served with Weygand on Foch's staff during the war. It was a short-lived government, lasting only until February 1930, but it was able to support Weygand's appointment.

The new war minister, André Maginot, who was to remain in office until his death, however, faced major political opposition difficulties. There was massive criticism from the Left, covertly directed against the proposed 1932 unification of the two appointments and overtly aimed personally against Weygand. Criticism of the unification of the posts claimed that a military dictatorship was being created by stealth and that the army's influence would be all-pervasive even if it did not have a military figure openly in charge of the government. For many on the Left even political neutrality was support for the existing establishment, which they desperately wanted to destroy. The personal attack on Weygand was vindictive. All the old suspicions and whispers reappeared: that he was a reactionary Catholic cavalry officer and a danger to the Republic; that he was of royal blood and his wife was an aristocrat; that he was bad-tempered, intolerant, and arrogant; that he was anti-German and anti-Soviet; and that he wanted a large and expensive army at a time when disarmament should be the aim of policy.[4]

Maginot was forced to make two significant concessions. The unfortunate Weygand was obliged to draft a statement to be read out by Maginot to the legislature.[5] The statement opened with Weygand's expressing that making such a statement was not in his character, but having been requested to do so he would speak. He went on to state that while he had been accused of political activity, he had never engaged in it, and that he had kept his ideas to himself and had had no dealings with anyone. But he wanted it to be known to those who were his chiefs that he was a Republican and that he could not imagine France with any regime other than a Republic. His statement concluded by affirming that he was a Catholic, but that he had never engaged in proselytizing, or in any of the military postings in which he had served had he ever inquired into the beliefs of those who served under his command, and he had always strived to be "fair." Maginot added that he was certain that a man such as General

Weygand would never speak out in disaccord with his conscience. It was an extraordinary requirement for a soldier being considered for a very senior office to have to make, and one viewed by Weygand with disgust.

The second condition, again with Weygand as much its target as a principle of a balanced command, was that Weygand should have the politically safe General Maurice Gamelin as an "assistant," and in 1932 when Pétain was due to retire, Weygand was to take his place as vice president of the CSG, enabling Gamelin to become chief of staff and also commander in chief in the event of war, a move that was to be of immense importance for the future. As it happened, Pétain moved to a new post, inspector general of air defense, and the second change took place in January 1931.

Such then were the domestic circumstances in which Weygand moved to the top posts in the French Army on January 3, 1930. He was now aged sixty-three.

Weygand's activities, values, and beliefs, conscious and unconscious, in the following five years can admit of widely different interpretations. Philip Bankwitz, in his impressively detailed, massively researched *Maxime Weygand and Civil-Military Relations in Modern France*, sees Weygand with his frequently expressed views on the disorder of France—the nation's political mediocrity, absence of social cohesion and discipline, valueless and unpatriotic education system—to be moving to a period of pessimistic cultural preparation for the installation of military rule. Although Weygand proclaimed loyalty to the Republic, was known to hate Nazism, and was not directly involved in any coup plotting, Bankwitz argues that he never spoke out against any of the militant right-wing groups and allowed himself, from a position of immense prestige and national admiration, to drift toward a view, perhaps subliminal until May 1940, that a military defeat might even be acceptable if it led to national regeneration. Perceived this way, Bankwitz claims, Weygand must take a large proportion of blame for the events of 1940.

Bernard Destremau, Weygand's French biographer, takes a different view. He sees the general as an increasingly lone voice bravely and repeatedly warning of the mounting dangers facing France. While not denigrating personal politicians of the Left who sought a defense policy based on disarmament, support for the League of Nations, and, if necessary, sanctions—views expressed by men who in several cases had distinguished war records—Weygand, according to Destremau, saw himself in a position of carrying great responsibility but being steadily deprived of real power and faced with ministers who simply did not want to know awkward facts. In his frustration, his past personal charm became increasingly replaced with outbursts of temper.

Several authors have written in favor of one or the other of these two theories. I would offer a third view. The imbalance of civil/military relations in France in these years had origins much further back in history than in the post-1918 politics of France. In their contemporary form, they were reflected in the deep fault line of mutual suspicion in France's national life opened by the passions of the Revolution and were visible in the passions evident in the *fiches* and Dreyfus affairs and the Clemenceau-Foch vendetta. In these circumstances, and in a France not yet recovered from her losses in the First World War, under very great economic strain, and facing again the German military menace, any solid agreement on civil/military balance was as likely as agreement over the politics of the guillotine during the Revolution. To single out an aged Weygand as a deliberate participant in an unfolding, inevitable tragedy leading to the national trauma of defeat is unjust. There could be no winners despite the honesty of the views held by many but not all of the leading actors; playing a personal blame game has little merit.

During this period both the international situation and domestic French politics could have hardly been less propitious. In Germany Hitler's star was now in the ascendant. It was clear that resentment over the Versailles Treaty, the 1920s inflation, unemployment, and for many the fear of the spread of communism was rousing a vengeful German nationalism. As early as 1927 the commander of the French Rhine Army, General Adolphe Guillaumat, had warned in a secret dispatch of the rising dangers to French security. There was also, approaching its peak in military technology before its erosion in the Spanish Civil War and wholesale obsolescence of the late 1930s, Mussolini's Italy with its constant refrain of "Tunis, Corsica, Nice." Finally, it was becoming more and more clear that the countries of Eastern Europe, sharply divided among themselves over local issues, would never continue to support France in a conflict against Germany or Italy, particularly if all that France was thinking about was defending its own frontier. Britain appeared to be primarily concerned over naval matters with Italy and Japan and was certainly not able to muster an effective land army without a long period of preparation. And Britain was often pursuing international policies opposed to those of France. Later, in 1936, Belgium would withdraw from its treaty with France, proclaiming a belief that strict neutrality would provide the better security.

The French military was tied up with pacification operations in Morocco, which lasted from 1929 to 1934 and involved over 60,000 men. In the view of many politicians, not only from the Right, the early cessation of these operations was needed. Due to the impact on the draft of the decline in the birth rate in the 1914–18 years, men could not be spared for African wars.

Successive events were to expose and deepen the French domestic fault line. In the five years of Weygand's service, January 1930 to January 1935, the rise and fall of fourteen prime ministers reflected the sharp political divisions. These years were the years of the Depression. Unemployment rose to 800,000, peaking at 1,000,000; trade, farming, and industry all suffered; family incomes fell; necessary social reforms had to be stopped. Leading political figures, notably Briand, envisaged a new, mutual disarmament and a friendly relationship with Germany; generals such as Weygand who remained suspicious of Berlin were viewed as obstructive.

In the cities, particularly Paris, public opinion moved from cynicism to exasperation with politicians, who were seen as self-seeking and corrupt. In consequence on each extreme, Right and Left, militant action groups appeared and grew in numbers. On the right the most important were the monarchist Action Française and a group that had begun in the 1920s as a harmless enough ex-servicemen's association, the Croix de Feu, which had by the mid-1930s, under its very passionate leader, Colonel Casimir de la Rocque, become neofascist. On the Left were the communists, the socialists, communist-led organized labor, and a number of others of the center Left who believed that communism might be preferable to a government of a Catholic and military establishment—or in some cases who saw the Left as the best route to power for themselves. Street clashes increased, and a crisis was to follow in Weygand's last year in office.

Amid this developing urban unrest there was less and less public concern for the state of the army; despite the accession to power of Hitler in 1933, antimilitarism remained strong. France's withdrawal from the occupation of the Rhineland and the ending of the Versailles Treaty supervision of the German army troubled few. The Maginot Line, for which the legislature voted large credits in January 1930, and static defense from Basel to Longwy (but not the Ardennes) was to be the national strategy. Little debate about other strategies or operational art took place. The armored-warfare theorists, in France Colonel Charles de Gaulle and very few others, were perceived by some as in advance of their time and by Weygand as divisive within the army if armor necessitated an all-professional force.[6] De Gaulle was considered to be troublesome, seeking controversy for himself. In the CSG there were personal rivalries within the bureaucracy and friction over the allocation of limited resources. New equipment if it arrived at all was often of poor quality. Pay was paltry; a French major still only earned about one-third of his British counterpart's pay. Morale was low and numbers fell. The 1932 Herriot government reduced the number of army officers by one-sixth, a policy as much political as economic.

The character weaknesses of General Gamelin, vagueness and imprecision, ambition and political attitudes that were to prove so fatal later on, were already evident. In the first months of their partnership, Gamelin played a waiting game with Weygand, but in fact he let it be known that he favored a strictly defensive strategy. In his defense, argued by Martin Alexander in his *The Republic in Danger: General Maurice Gamelin and the Politics of French Defence 1933–1940,* Gamelin saw the defensive strategy and maintenance of close ties with politicians as a necessary compromise, the best that could be achieved in the political climate of the 1930s. He was, however, too prone to present as anti-Republican, those right-wing extremists who persistently continued to sound the alarm.[7]

After the changeover, Weygand soon found (it would seem to his surprise and certainly resentment) that in the contemporary political climate the balance of power between the vice president of the CSG and the chief of staff had changed, and that he was the loser.

While Weygand's thinking still did not go as far as that of the extreme armored-warfare exponents, he drew on his experience of the autumn of 1918: penetrate the enemy's line of defense and keep on the move to prevent the enemy from organizing further defenses. He recognized that the armored army would have to be professional, a notion too powerful for French politicians ever to accept. His aim for the French Army was to restore its morale and self-confidence and to provide it with an adequate supply of draft conscripts and the equipment and fuel for a motorized army capable of rapid movement. He was not to receive full support, from either Pétain above or Gamelin below, the weak support from the latter becoming evident soon after the 1931 changeover.

The three prime ministers that followed the Left's return to power from June 1932 to October 1933—Edouard Herriot, Joseph Paul-Boncour, and Edouard Daladier—all disliked Weygand, Boncour's dislike amounting to hatred. All three were faced with the worst period of the Depression and the increasing street activities of the various factions. The last of the three, Daladier, fell from power in October 1933 and was replaced by the very short lived regimes of Albert Sarraut and Camille Chautemps. He returned to power briefly in January 1934, before his government collapsed amid bloodshed and violence in the following month.

Weygand himself remained true to the pillar of his beliefs, continuing to argue, with now perhaps a measure of tension from his own origins, for a strong and effective French army as essential for security. He campaigned for this with increasingly intemperate passion. Politicians and ministers saw him as beyond control, which merely intensified Weygand's already quite negative view of politicians. He became less prudent, while harboring serious doubts (which would prove correct) over whether a proper balance between a civil government and its military could be realized before it was too late. In opposition to him, political leaders clung with equal passion and patriotism to visions, reflecting both France's 1870 and 1914–18 experiences and the contemporary economic situation, that political control over the military must be maintained and that in any case security was adequately maintained by the Maginot Line.[8]

Weygand cannot carry the full blame for France's failure to recognize and respond to the growing threat from Germany. He could see clearly and correctly the emerging dangers, but he was faced with an ever-changing succession of political leaders unable to agree on much more than denial of those dangers. The more moderate ones were concerned with national budgets, others further to the left with their more radical, and to Weygand destructive, plans for the professional army. But all were living in a comfortable delusion of the possibility for international agreement and general disarmament, an illusion that a Catholic traditional general could not hope to break.

The rift between these camps in the early 1930s was becoming not just one of simple sharp disagreement but one in which neither side could muster any empathy for the other. Complete breakdown was to follow in 1934. After a fifteen month period of cooperation, the return in June 1932 of Herriot as prime minister raised the incendiary issue of disarmament. One left-wing cry to be heard was "Shoot a French general not a foreign soldier."

Weygand was acutely aware that the military balance following rapid German rearmament was turning to serious French disadvantage. Almost fanatically, he disputed with Herriot that Germany was a country one could deal with or trust in any mutually balanced force-reduction program. He urged a reoccupation of the Rhineland and opposed the work of the International Geneva Conference and disarmament planners, while the political Left was divided and unable to produce a credible, coherent alternative strategy. Weygand apparently hinted at but it seems did not openly threaten resignation. Pétain supported Weygand but not very effectively.

To Weygand's great disappointment and resentment, Gamelin had begun to adjust his views toward the political establishment, asserting that the League of Nations would provide security. In the streets Weygand was not helped by support from de la Rocque and the Croix de Feu, which only gave the Left and politicians calling for his replacement an additional weapon with which to attack him in the press. In the event, amid the difficult and irreconcilable conditions sought by negotiators at the Geneva Conference, the cause of disarmament lost momentum after the Doumergue National Union French government rejected a British proposal for arms limitation and control in March 1934, the continuous pressure applied by Weygand having had its effect on the new administration even if it had largely failed with its predecessors. The whole issue finally came to an end after Weygand's retirement in 1936 when the Geneva Conference collapsed following unacceptable German demands.

The second major issue was one of manpower. The Depression was at its height, and the government was desperate to reduce costs. Weygand faced a situation in which, in his own words, the army was being reduced to a "façade," with divisions and regiments reduced to 30, sometimes even 40, percent below strength and unable to man Maginot's planned defenses. The government and Weygand in particular also had to face the big fall in the number of eighteen-year-old conscripts after 1934, resulting from the 1914–18 war casualties. Successive governments sought to patch this over by reducing the length of service by two months and through other local regional arrangements. Weygand believed that these policies were only temporary measures and judged that he had been tricked when he found they were to be lasting. He was also angry at the promotion of officers whom he thought to be mediocre but who held "safe" political views; he believed that this was all part of a plan by the Left to destroy the professional army. His protests, even one to President Albert Lebrun, were rejected or ignored, and when support at a December 1933 C S G meeting gained his views a majority, they were overruled by Daladier, then war minister, in the legislature the following day. His two military successes in these years within his eight-year moderation program were the conversion of a cavalry division into a light mechanized division and the preparation for four motorized infantry divisions together with a very limited order for the improved and excellent B1 heavy tank. He was also sent to Morocco on a visit in late 1933, ostensibly to report on the final stages of military occupation operations, but probably covertly to remove him from the scene for a brief period. He was, though, able to defend the local military against further political criticism.

At the end of 1933 the very questionable financial dealings of a trader of Ukrainian Jewish ancestry, Serge Stavisky, already under police investigation, became exposed after revelations concerning a massive fraud. Stavisky had influential social and political connections within the Left establishment who had until this major scandal protected him, but were incapable of any further hushing up. Of his protectors one was a government minister; another was the public prosecutor, a brother-in-law of the then prime minister Chautemps. Faced with ruin, Stavisky and his mistress committed suicide in January 1934. A torrent of political invective opened up from the Right accusing the political leaders of involvement in Stavisky's shady dealings and attempts at a cover-up. Chautemps was forced to resign and his place taken by Daladier, who on February 6 was faced with a massive 40,000-strong demonstration of right-wing action groups led by Colonel de la Rocque's Croix de Feu and supported by the Action Française together with the militant anticommunist Jeunesses Patriotes. These turned to violent street battles in which sixteen people were killed and a large number of policemen were injured. Parliamentarians fled when the legislature was threatened. Daladier resigned and a respected former president, Gaston Doumergue, formed a "National Government" that included Pétain as war minister. A tense day followed on the 9th when the organizations of the Left mounted a rival massive demonstration in eastern Paris, claiming with justification that elements in the demonstration of the 6th were planning a coup. There was further but greatly reduced bloodshed before this demonstration was dispersed and some measure of order restored.

Amid this turmoil, Weygand, who had returned from the south of France, was preparing for the contingency of declaring military emergency powers. But his reappearance set off rumors that he was to be the key figure in a right-wing coup or even that he and Marshal Lyautey, another bogeyman for the Left, would lead one. His sympathies would certainly have been with the political Right, among whom he had many friends, but also among whom he must have been aware there were sharp divisions. He must also have been aware that his *chef du cabinet,* Colonel Jean de Lattre de Tassigny, the future Marshal, had contacts with some of the right-wing groups, though he may well not have known that de Lattre was presenting himself as from Weygand's staff. Later Weygand scuppered Pétain's demand to replace de Lattre by issuing an order and ensuring that it was never carried out. He had no sympathy for the government or any desire to help it, but he took no action personally against it, retaining an entirely correct attitude. And as a soldier he would have seen that any military action other than restoring order would have caused splits within the army.

The events of February 6, 1934, can be seen as the major turning point for civil-military relations in France. To this date the balance among the parties had been maintained, albeit very precariously, by periodic changes of government and some restraint by both sides. An all-out rift had been avoided, despite pressure from the Left, thanks to the interludes provided by the regimes of Poincaré and Tardieu and the support Maginot received from Painlevé. Weygand may have covertly assisted in preparing arguments that appeared in journal articles written by others, but the possibility of a civil-military rupture had now become an issue of national survival. Politicians continued to argue for their ultimate supremacy as essential for a true Republic and to represent the will of the voters. Despite their internal divisions, they moved toward the hard-left coalition of Léon Blum's 1936 Popular Front government, in turn to be claimed by some as the vanguard of a communist coup. But the divisions among them left the whole system weak, to be shaken further by uncertain views over the growing menace of Nazi Germany, which now worried many ordinary people, particularly in the middle classes and some in the military, shaken by the performance of German forces in Spain. Others began to wonder whether a politically correct military leader might not be the best solution. The possible costs and the continuing wider public dislike of the army—any form of conscription rarely produces wide enthusiasm for the military—were, however, constraining.

The army itself also had internal divisions. Many of the old "establishment" officers had left in despair; younger officers, worried by German rearmament and the Popular Front, supported the idea of a military leader. Many also feared communism. The defensive military strategy was frustrating and contrary to the temperament of the best and most active officers. Leaflets, articles, and books from the political Right lent support.

Theorists, some influenced by German writers and generals, began saying that the army, as the true permanent soul of the nation, representing all that was healthy and disciplined in society, and as the guardian of the nation, was perhaps in a special position to arbitrate between the Right and Left, provided the civil-military balance tilted in favor of the military. There were dark, fevered, and endless reports and rumors of plotted coups and revolutions by militant activists on both sides and hints of Weygand as a potential leader among those of the Right. Whatever his private sympathies may have been and despite personal approaches made to him, Weygand never indicated any support for such projects. Whatever mental turmoil he may have suffered as events unfolded—the Nazi "Night of Long Knives," the German entry into the Rhineland, the annexation of Austria, the Sudetenland crisis—his conduct remained true to the declaration made by Maginot on his behalf in 1929.

Weygand was bitterly disappointed that the Doumergue government collapsed in November 1934. It had, however, extended the length of national service to two years and checked the proposed retirement of a large number of officers. Weygand was due to retire in February 1935 and was for a brief period freed from much criticism and hostility. He was known to oppose negotiations with the Soviet Union; he had expressed some admiration for Mussolini, still at this time a leader held in general respect by both Britain and France; and he later followed this with a guarded respect for General Franco. He drew closer to Pétain with total contempt for the Republic in its current form, but he still preferred that it should be renewed and revitalized without a formal revolution, and anyway he was no longer to be in the midst. For the political leaders there could still be no question: Republican civil authority must prevail over the military; the balance could not be tilted. Later, during and after 1940, many were to argue that military pressures on the frail and divided political leadership inhibited military preparations and provided Hitler with encouragement in his belief that France could be defeated.

Weygand could not adequately grasp the impossibility of a change from the views of political leaders in the political climate of post-1918 France. It is easy to criticize the limits of his vision, but there was also a dimension that in turn political leaders could never fully understand. A general is a man in uniform charged with the lives of fellow men who have to obey him. His beliefs in peace and his strategy and orders in war can send many hundreds of men loyal to him to their deaths. His is a very direct field responsibility, very different from that of a distant political leader and one that can weigh heavily, particularly on a man such as Weygand who had had experience of the burdens of command and was devoted to the army. To these different views must be added, on both sides, the personal ambitions of the leading actors, though here, with confidence Weygand can be exempted.

Weygand was now to enjoy three and a half years of retirement before being ordered back to a national responsibility. In these years when he was technically still retained on the active list on full pay, though not employed, Weygand engaged in private correspondence with political leaders and in much military journal and newspaper article writing on the state of the army, but he still never advocated any form of military intervention.

It again came to be argued that his frustrations and pessimism in those years served as a further form of mental preparation for military intervention, but no clear evidence of any such psychological operation exists. He still hoped that the attack of a superior German army could eventually be contained by properly trained and equipped defensive systems together with, when opportunity so presented, limited motorized counterattack and eventually a major 1918-style counteroffensive. He believed de Gaulle's advocacy of an armored force now contained an additional hitherto unrecognized disadvantage in that it would create divisions and undermine cohesion within the army. Weygand also still appeared to have little idea of the effect of aircraft development on direct ground fighting. He remained worried about France's industrial capacity, about the provision of fuel for motorized units, and in particular about the apparent lack of élan and professional pride among conscripts.

His alarm over what he saw as a moral failure led Weygand to express views on education in a book published in 1937, *Comment élever nos fils*. He had himself brought his two sons up very firmly but also with a real family affection that he himself had never had. In 1939 the elder, Edouard, was a promising engineer, the younger, Jacques, an army captain noted and decorated for his professional ability and service in Morocco. Weygand saw the national education system as lacking an ethos, preoccupied with formal examinations, and taught in old buildings by teachers, not always of ability, who imposed long hours of work on pupils. Physical education was neglected, and above all the whole system was lacking in the teaching of integrity and patriotism, an absence very evident when the students became adults.[9]

Although he never directly intervened within the military or directly criticized Gamelin, his views on the French military scene were clearly enough expressed in another small book, *La France, est-elle défendue?*, also published in 1937, in which he set out in much more detail the imbalance of German and French forces and warned of the dangers of sudden attack.[10] He was taken to task by the political Left, in particular over his now strong opposition to any form of military cooperation and discussions with the Soviet Union. Weygand, aware of Berlin's earlier secret military contacts with Moscow and fearful of the formation of the emergence of a German-Russian military alliance against France, had therefore at first been cautiously supportive of cooperation with Moscow, but when discussions ended he turned to outright opposition. He was later accused of hypocrisy over this change, and after 1945 it was argued that the absence of Soviet military intervention was a cause of the collapse of France in 1940, an accusation that hardly accorded with the realities of Soviet military power in May 1940. The Left later even went so far as to allege that his opposition was a major reason for Stalin's turning toward an agreement with Hitler.

Weygand would no doubt have had Poland much in mind from his experienced assessment that if the Red Army entered Poland the country would be again partitioned and *finis Poloniae*. For a second anti-German front he favored the Balkans, but essentially he did not think any second front necessary. As with many other senior officers he continued to believe a citizen militia army, still much favored by many on the Left, would be fatal. He continued to be considered by many to be France's best military brain. It can certainly be claimed that if his views had been taken in the years when he was in power, 1930–34, and even on to the German reentry into the Rhineland in 1936, France could have done more than survive a German onslaught, even perhaps effecting the fall of Hitler. By the late 1930s, though, the correlation of population and military strength was fast turning to France's very serious disadvantage, and in the French military, an air of unreality, in which Weygand was far less culpable than Gamelin, had set in fatally.

France was bitterly divided. The Left still opposed any full rearmament. The Blum Popular Front government had been brought down by the power of financial interests. The communists saw the approaching war as one between capitalist interests that were to be confronted and destroyed in order to create a Soviet state. Strikes targeted key industries. On the Right many sought a Franco-German rapprochement. Some were assisted in this argument with support from antiwar societies and the increasingly influential Comité France-Allemagne funded covertly from Berlin; others, particularly in industry, saw the production of motor cars as far more preferable than the production of tanks. Some major business and commercial interests published their own newssheets; a few supported the hooded *Cagoulards* or other neofascist militias hoping for a day when an authoritarian regime could be installed. The cry "Better Hitler than

Blum" was to be heard on the Right, while on the Left major capitalists were denounced as the *gros légumes*. The divisions disgusted Weygand. He remained a stanch conservative but was never a neofascist.

In the final prewar months Weygand's views seemed to become confused, out of touch, and incoherent. He now accepted the need for a nucleus professional army to work in parallel with a mainly conscript force, and, fearing a surprise German land and air attack on the north and the south flanks of the Maginot Line, he saw an important use of French tanks as a mobile artillery force available to contain such an attack. The Spanish Civil War had alerted him to the new threats from the air. Although successive French governments, alarmed at the growing strength of Germany, had authorized increases in military expenditure, Weygand at times saw himself increasingly as a lone voice crying in the wilderness for a properly equipped army and air force. He opposed as appeasement the 1938 Munich agreement welcomed by Georges Bonnet, the foreign minister who opposed rearmament and disliked the British. At other times he seemed concerned that exposing the serious weaknesses within the French Army would simply encourage his country's enemies. He may have had some sympathies with a few of the military views of the new militant right-wing *Cagoulards,* but he was never associated with their activities. Weygand's relationship with de Gaulle, between a lieutenant colonel and a senior general, was at this time one of mutual regard but continuing theoretical disagreement. Any meetings the two had were purely casual, but there was no indication whatever of the later mutual hostility.

In his personal life Weygand took much pleasure in his membership in the Académie Française, to which he was elected in 1931 and formally admitted in 1932. His literary credentials were based upon his biography of Henri de la Tour d'Auvergne, vicomte de Turenne. His address on his formal reception was a eulogy of Joffre, to whose place, Seat 35, in the Académie he had been voted. He spoke also of Turenne and Foch developing themes of offensive-defense and the need for prompt pursuit, respected by Turenne but well-practiced by Foch. While accepting an overall civilian political general direction, he began to attest, as had Foch, that field military commanders were not simple executives of a civil authority but must be allowed full powers of initiative in operations to ensure victory.

In 1938, after some eighteen months of cautious reediting, his *Histoire de l'Armée Française* appeared.[11] It is a relatively short work, just under four hundred pages. Weygand's emphasis was more on organization and weapons than on accounts of campaigns and battles, but linked with praise for Napoleon's military genius and ability to unite France. The main themes that he struck were France's total dependence on its army for security and the unifying, binding role of the army for society as a whole. He emphasized the dangers of a defensive strategy, particularly if the country did not have the necessary material immediately to hand when faced with a sudden attack, the need for a strong government, and national patriotism. He expressed his doubts on the value of colonial regiments for the modern defense of the *métropole*. With prescience he feared enemy propaganda attacks on the loyalty of colonial regiments. While he admired the service rendered by French colonial soldiers in the First World War, he foresaw African or Indochinese soldiers might return home to use their military skills and perhaps weapons against their colonial rulers. Later, in the period of post-1940 recrimination, critics of Weygand were to allege that his military history writings all reflected a latent authoritarianism, but there is little justification for this.

Weygand also continued with his wider interests in arts and literature, and traveled, seeing his visits to foreign countries as a temporary escape from his anxieties over the international scene. He became an administrator of the Suez Canal Company, traveling to Egypt, where he met King Fuad. He represented France at the marriage of the son of the shah of Iran, the future Reza Shah, to a daughter of the king of Egypt. He visited Romania and Turkey, with a diplomatic agenda, and met with King Carol and Marshal Fevzi Çakmak, attempting to interest them in problems of security. King Carol expressed his fear of Germany and communism. Other travels included further visits to Spain, Gibraltar, and Morocco.

In the summer of 1939 he visited Britain. The visit included spending a day at the Royal Military College Sandhurst and viewing the (one and only) tank brigade on exercise. He left the brigade shaking his head and remarking to the General Officer Commanding, Southern Command, that he hoped Britain really had something better than what he had been shown, though he appeared doubtful. The visit almost certainly left an impression, to be recalled in the following year.[12]

The crisis of August 1939 saw Weygand, now seventy-two and, despite some recent kidney trouble, still very fit. His contemporaries did note that he had often become much more irritable and intolerant, reminiscent of his bearing during the 1919 Versailles conference period. He retained his custom of rising early and riding most mornings, always immaculately turned out, and he put in a long day of activities. He saw himself ready for, and was hoping for, a return to active service in the event of war.

Later in the month the Daladier government sent him back to Syria and Lebanon as commander in chief of French forces in the Levant.[13] Upon receiving this appointment he resigned from the Suez Canal Company administration. The French government had become concerned with growing German interest in the Balkans, in particular with reports of military and air cooperation with Bulgaria. It was thought that the dispatch of a prestigious military figure would affirm French interest in the area. Weygand's biographer believes that the support given to this decision by Gamelin was also motivated by Gamelin's wish to have Weygand well out of the way. It may also have included a wish to test the old general's physical robustness for command.

Weygand's mission was twofold. First was to consult with the governments of Turkey, Greece, and Romania and to try to broker an agreement for mutual support with them. Only Turkey was prepared to risk a formal agreement in face of German wrath. Weygand also worked with the British Middle East commander in chief, General Sir Archibald Wavell, renewing a friendship formed earlier in Gibraltar. Wavell was in accord with Weygand's activities but had to remain cautious in view of the likelihood of a Libya-based attack by Italy on Egypt. Weygand's mission was limited by French inability to supply arms and equipment, but he did believe that in a war conducted in alliance with Britain against the Italians only, and not including the Germans, success could be assumed.

Weygand's second task was to prepare a military force capable of effective intervention. The garrison on his arrival in the Levant consisted of two understrength, underequipped brigades: one of West-African Tirailleurs of little use in a Balkan winter, the other of locally recruited Alawite units. This scratch force was reinforced by a properly equipped full-strength Armée d'Afrique division with tanks and modern artillery, which had arrived from Algeria in October. In the words of Weygand himself they constituted a force "far removed from the least flattering estimates of what the newspapers and propaganda called 'The Weygand Army.'" These were months of illusion. Was it realistic to suggest that such a force could land and operate from Salonika and that there could also be a British landing on the Gallipoli peninsula and perhaps even a landing in Crete by the French from Algeria?

Both of Weygand's tasks also involved much unrewarding correspond-ence with Paris, local visits of inspection, and supervision of training, but neither Daladier nor Gamelin kept him informed on the situation and events in France.

An even wilder illusion was a project planned by Gamelin and Admi-ral François Darlan for the preparation of airfields in Syria for bombing missions on Soviet oil installations at Batum and Baku in the Caucasus. Turkey was not to be consulted over the use of its air space. Funds for this work were confirmed by Prime Minister Paul Reynaud on April 27, 1940, with a few modern aircraft arriving in May; construction plans for the airfield were immediately set in hand. Weygand apparently approved of this senseless project on the grounds that it would weaken Germany.[14] Completion of the project was to be overtaken by events.

The total absence of reality in the Levant policy in many ways high-lights the wider French situation. Before the passionate views of the dif-ferent actors, Right and Left, military and civil, lay the divisive gulf of the 1790s. Faced with the impossibility of any realistic agreement, opinions were reduced to a public *je m'en fous* shrug of the shoulders or acquies-cence in denying reality with the phrase, widespread in the earliest days of the war, "We shall win because we are the strongest."

CODA

During the liberation of Paris in August 1944 a member of General Jacques Leclerc's 2nd Armored Division fired a shell from his tank gun into the façade of the Palais Bourbon, the French Parliament building. Asked to explain himself he replied, "I have been wanting to do this for the last fifteen years."

5

≕+ ≕+ ≕+

COMMANDER IN CHIEF
MAY–JUNE 1940

It was still just possible that if France had entered the Second World War with the national resolve of 1914 the outcome of events might have been very different. If the French Army, even if not armored but at least motorized, had immediately sallied forth from the Maginot fortresses in effective support for Poland, the Nazi regime and the German Army would have faced grave problems, with serious fighting on two fronts and areas of Germany occupied by the French. The 1938 static defensive strategy, however, precluded such action, and in the severe 1939–40 winter two events took place that were to make French defeat inevitable. In September 1939 there had been a measure of motivation in the war even among reluctant recalled reservists and despite the political disinterest or outright opposition of the extreme Left. The long, very cold 1939–40 winter, though, sapped the morale of recalled reservists, who saw little purpose in their uninspiring daily routines; undermined by continuing antiwar and left-wing propaganda, morale slumped. Daladier's banning of the French Communist Party in September 1939 had further enraged the Left but was an inevitable consequence of the August 1939 German-Russian agreement. At the same time the Germans had made a careful study of the lessons of the Polish campaign, developing aircraft communication with armored units and improved command and control of tank subunits and individual machines to precision.

On paper the ground forces joined in battle on May 10, 1940, did not seem hopelessly unbalanced. The Germans were able to field 133 divisions,

of which 10 were armored assault formations, together with older tanks
in many of the infantry divisions. The Allied armies totaled 145 divisions: 10 Dutch, 22 Belgian, a 102 French, and 9 British, these latter not
including 3 without artillery employed on lines-of-communication duties. Among these divisions France had four very newly formed armored
divisions, of which three had virtually no formation training, and one
British division with regiments never to be assembled together. In the
air the Germans had a very large lead: 4,200 aircraft compared with the
Anglo-French total of 1,400 French and 416 British machines, most ill-
suited for coordinated action with ground troops. Further, twelve of the
French infantry divisions were very largely formed of North African men,
and eight more had a high percentage of West African men, together with
others, including Malagasies serving in the Maginot Line's forty divisions. Most but not all of the divisions that included West Africans were
posted on the Italian frontier (where later in June 1940 they were to fight
well), but North and West African troops, with nothing more than machine guns with which to combat German tanks and aircraft, inevitably
proved of diminishing value.

At the top French command arrangements were grotesquely disor-
dered. Gamelin, supposedly in Supreme Allied Command, had his headquarters at Vincennes. Forty miles away at La Ferté-sous-Jouarre was the
headquarters of the very able but medically far from fit General Alphonse
Georges, at the time the commander in chief North East France, but soon
to be promoted to be Weygand's deputy. A further important headquarters for French Army land forces headed by General André Doumenc
was at Montry on the Marne. The air force commander, General Joseph
Vuillemin, was at a fourth location, Coulonniers.

These separate ground force locations reflected Gamelin's style, a preference for the company of dutiful staff officers rather than the troubles
of dealing with subordinate generals who might hold ideas differing from
his own. He particularly disliked Georges and so kept him at a distance.
Gamelin remained an intellectual figure, dispensing ideas and philo-
sophic concepts and devolving responsibility to others rather than issuing
clear-cut orders. Though exceedingly intelligent and aware of the strength
of his enemy, he never exercised proper supervision over operations or
training. From as early as September 9, Gamelin had fixed in his mind that

the main German offensive would be through Belgium.[1] In particular he discarded intelligence reports that had warned him of German plans to attack through Sedan and the Ardennes, sidestepping the Maginot Line, believing that the French Ninth and Second Armies could contain any assault in terrain assessed as impassable for armor. For the longer-term future he thought a French counteroffensive in 1941, or more likely 1942, would be possible. Denying reality, he lived in a mental world of his own imagining, a sad, irresolute, overambitious, but for all of his faults patriotic, officer.

In sum, neither the French command nor the morale state of many (but certainly not all) French divisions was in an adequate condition to meet the well-equipped and commanded, battle-experienced, and highly motivated German army. The command's problems were to be inherited by Weygand, soon only too well aware of them, in ten days after the opening of the German assault.

This massive German armor, parachute, and glider troop assault began early in the morning of May 10. By the 19th the Dutch had capitulated. The French Seventh and First Armies, composed of the best units of the French Army and the British Expeditionary Force, had been pushed back westward from the line of the Dyle-Breda, which Gamelin had intended to hold, to the Escaut. The Germans had crossed the Meuse both at Dinant and more importantly at Sedan, with indications that they planned to scythe west and cut off the Allies in north France and Belgium rather than move south toward Paris.

On the morning of May 17 Captain Gasser, Weygand's military aide, handed Weygand a secret telegram from the prime minister, Paul Reynaud, ordering him to return to Paris immediately, giving no reasons. Weygand's journey in a bomber aircraft was delayed by bad weather, necessitating a stopover at a British Army garrison officers' mess at Mersa Matruh in Egypt. On his arrival in France the undercarriage of the aircraft gave way, and exit from the machine was difficult. Weygand had been warned in advance by the French Resident in Beirut that Reynaud wanted to replace Gamelin and could have had no illusions about the reason for his recall when he arrived on the 19th. Reynaud, an overburdened and essentially weak man, first ordered him to visit Gamelin and Georges and then to report back in the evening. Weygand found Gamelin expecting to be relieved, Georges suffering and fatigued, and the staffs of both men deeply depressed. When Weygand returned for his meeting with Reynaud, he found the prime minister accompanied significantly by Marshal Pétain, whom Reynaud had appointed deputy prime minister. The pair formally asked Weygand if he was willing to replace Gamelin. A man of Weygand's temperament and sense of loyalty could hardly refuse. He replied that he was willing to assume the responsibility but that the prime minister should not be surprised if he was not able to deliver a victory. The transfer of command followed, Gamelin providing an overview that was far from complete. To this point Weygand had little idea of the events of the previous ten days. In Beirut he had not been kept properly informed, probably deliberately; earlier reports from Gamelin had been unrealistic and optimistic. The day ended with a service of national prayer at Notre-Dame Cathedral, a service of great meaning and importance for Weygand but less so for Pétain, Reynaud, and other politicians.

In consideration of the tumultuous events that followed, four issues may usefully be borne in mind. First, faced with a situation that still appeared with real determination possible to retrieve, did Weygand, as a former chief of staff and now for the first time in his life in actual command of very large forces, make the correct decisions and battle plans when he took over command? Second, the duty of any military leader from corporal to field marshal is to inspire men to efforts for which they never believed they were capable by the style of his leadership, and as important, he must maintain, in Lord Wavell's words, "robustness" and calm in adversities. Did Weygand provide such inspiration and calm, or could he, or anyone, in the situation in which he found himself, have ever provided it? Third, what should a commander in chief, responsible to his government both for his nation's renown and for the lives of several thousands of soldiers and many more in the civil population, decide to do when faced with catastrophic defeat, one that was clearly irreversible? Four, does what the commander in chief himself decide to do with his own person matter? Such questions were not studied at staff colleges.

In answer to the first, Weygand, although only chief of staff, had learned how to plan battles from his master, Foch. His plans were excellent, but the inferiority of the Allied armies, in face of superior German forces, precluded success for his or anyone else's plans. Second, despite his prestige, Weygand lacked the charisma of Foch. He was able to motivate those immediately around him by his personality, still vigorous and alive, but he had little impact on the mass of soldiers, whose attitude was to become increasingly one of "I am prepared to die if there was some purpose for it, but we are lost already and I am not prepared to give my life to no purpose." Further, as the military situation worsened to crisis point, Weygand was able to remain robust and calm only when making military decisions. Faced with a political leadership for which from the very beginning he had little respect, calm went and tempers were to flare.

In the third issue Weygand was to put as his priority his perception of his army's and his country's honor, and the lives of his soldiers, together with the social cohesion of his country. Events in his own lifetime were in his mind. He had seen that in October–November 1918 the German surrender had directly saved thousands of German soldiers' lives and the German heartland from becoming a battlefield, and also indirectly saved Germany from a Leninist revolution, all on the basis of a deal by which political leaders, including socialists, preserved the army. His choice of actions was, however, contrary to established legal civil-military relations and would arouse controversy. Fourth, even if the "verdict of history" upon him personally was not one of his concerns, the future of his person as a national figure had to be considered. A prolonged campaign that ended with a defeat so total that the nation and the wider world would see Marshal Pétain and himself either marched off as German prisoners of war or forced into exile abroad could have wide and lasting consequences for the army and for France. For both of these two issues the alternative of a timely emergency assertion of military authority over a discredited political order seemed to become the only option that might salvage something from the wreckage of defeat and provide opportunities for recovery in time, as later Weygand was to attempt and much later use to justify himself.

The first three weeks following Weygand's appointment were to be the most important and controversial in his own and his country's twentieth-century history. Some of the pages of the detailed account that follows will make distressing reading.[2] Weygand's arrival in command was greeted with much public enthusiasm, a belief that like Joffre he would snatch victory from defeat and then like Foch lead the Allies to victory, a public denial of the reality, which was nothing but an impediment. To show his staff that the chief of staff of 1918 had not lost personal vigor he ran a 100-meter sprint a few times before watching officers, but May 1940 was not September 1914. From the start Weygand's problems were complicated by a personal dislike and mistrust of Reynaud, reciprocated by Reynaud's dislike of him. Further, Reynaud, although combative, was dominated by his mistress, the glamorous but sinister Comtesse Hélène de Portes.

Now in command, Weygand directed that as an emergency measure ordnance stock of the famous 75mm World War I–era field gun be opened up so that the guns might be used as antitank artillery, for which, however, the proper ammunition had not even been designed, and that the roads of northern France be cleared of the masses of terrified refugees streaming south, an order that was largely impractical to implement.

Later in the day he moved his staff to Montry, where he was given a full briefing on the gravity of the situation by the very able and clear-thinking Doumenc, including some serious facts that Gamelin had not given him. Faced with the reality, Weygand was stupefied. He still believed, though, that it was possible that all might not be lost and that the prime need was to revitalize the energies of subordinate commanders, who were either basking in warm May sun or not yet recovered from the shock of earlier defeat. He and Doumenc correctly saw the operational need must be the mounting of simultaneous attacks from north and south on the German scythe sweeping toward the Channel. He was unaware of the failure of the French army's initial attempts to prevent encirclement in Belgium and the north. The new attacks in the north, although now cut off, were now to be made by the elite divisions of the 1st French Army Group and the British. The fewer units on the south and south of the Somme were not of the same quality. To strengthen them Weygand asked that the general reserve formations be committed—but was told that there were none and munitions stocks were running out. Further, all communications were difficult, many headquarters had no wireless, and civilian telephone lines were broken or cut.

To develop the pincer project Weygand planned an early visit to see General Gaston Billotte, commanding the 1st Army Group in Belgium and northern France on the north side of the scythe, with whom communication was proving especially difficult, often possible only via London. Billotte's army group had originally been deployed west to east with four French armies, the Seventh under General Henri Giraud, then the BEF, the First Army under Georges Blanchard, the Eighth under André Corap, and the Second under Charles Huntziger, together with the Belgians, whose king, Leopold III, Weygand also hoped to see. But by this time Corap's army of particularly poor-quality recalled reservists had been largely destroyed, that of Huntziger was in little better shape, and Henri Giraud, who had replaced Corap in command of what was left of the Ninth Army, had been taken prisoner.

Early on May 21 Weygand according left Doumenc's headquarters and flew north to a deserted airstrip northwest of Béthune, surviving spasmodic German anti-aircraft fire and with only a disheveled and dirty soldier on the ground to receive him.[3] On the way from his vantage point squatting in the aircraft's corridor and later traveling on the roads, he could see the start of the tragic refugee chaos—men, women, and children, some in cars or carts, others trudging on foot, fleeing the German advance, their numbers already in the hundreds of thousands and increasing each day, jamming the roads and being occasionally machine-gunned by German aircraft. Of Billotte or King Leopold there was no sign. The lone soldier at the airstrip acquired an old Ford delivery van, which he drove with Weygand and two staff officers in the back to a local township that still had a working telephone. From there they moved on to Ypres, where Weygand was joined by senior Belgian politicians and military officers; the king arrived soon after and sometime later, Billotte. There was, however, neither any sign nor news of the BEF Commander John, Lord Gort, who had had to turn his attention to a crisis on the British front and to the likelihood of an evacuation by sea. Weygand suspected that this was a calculated snub and that Gort had his own designs.

Weygand saw his plans as vital. The best 1st Army Group divisions, including the four motorized formations, although cut off, he believed still retained combat power. For the southern component of his pincer attack, he hoped the hurriedly assembled group of second-class divisions could participate, or at least hold the front. For this plan, though, the Belgian army would be required to withdraw southward and westward to protect the flank of the combined French and British attack. The Belgian commander in chief, General Raoul Van Overstraeten, objected to another large area of Belgium being left to the Germans, and the king supported him, both claiming the Belgian army was already exhausted and in no condition for a major withdrawal; the king appeared defeatist. Weygand hoped that the arrival of the British Admiral Sir Roger Keyes, attached to King Leopold's staff, might lead to a change of mind, and he vetoed the Belgian plan. General Billotte, probably the ablest of the French field commanders, then arrived and endorsed Weygand's plan; of Gort there was still no sign.[4]

At this point Admiral Jean Abrial arrived with the news that an aircraft journey back to Paris for Weygand, who was supposed to report daily to Reynaud, was now out of the question and that he would have to make a hazardous road journey to Dunkirk, where a small French destroyer would take him under cover of night to Cherbourg, via Dover. Weygand undertook the night journey, the destroyer leaving Dunkirk under heavy air attack. As it happened, after disembarking at Cherbourg, Weygand received some much needed briefing on the realities of the situation during the railway journey to Paris from three French staff officers who had been sent to meet him. Back at Ypres, the exhausted Billotte was left to explain and coordinate Weygand's plan with Gort, who arrived sometime after Weygand's departure. The plan's already limited chances of success, however, suffered an additional disastrous setback. During the night Billotte was involved in a motor car accident from which he died without recovering consciousness; the written notes he left behind were concerned only with movements on the French stock exchange.

On arrival back in Paris, Weygand, weary and unshaven but with some unwise optimism, reported to Reynaud and Pétain and later met the new British prime minister, Winston Churchill, his first meeting with Churchill since the First World War years. All approved his plan, Churchill promising full Royal Air Force support, as did later the same day Leopold, at this point still keeping his reservations to himself. Weygand noted, at this stage with only mild concern, that Churchill had received a report that German troops had been seen at Etaples, near the coast south of Boulogne, and that Gort was concentrating his efforts on his seaward right flank, understandably in view of his need to maintain links with his supply ports but also a move open to other interpretations.

Weygand also took note that the Royal Air Force was now withdrawing to Britain and refusing to base its fighter force in France, offering only sweeps launched from bases in south England. In the next two days, Weygand's mild concern turned to suspicion. Gort openly began a withdrawal toward Dunkirk in order to preserve his right flank. From the Channel ports reports reached Weygand that British stores were being returned to France, and there did not appear to be any great effort by the Royal Air Force. Weygand could not help contrasting the size of the BEF, nine divisions as opposed to the sixty present in 1918, and despite his admiration for the British soldier, wondering how seriously the United Kingdom was committed to the war.

In view of Reynaud's strict instructions, Weygand now decided that he must remain near Paris for daily briefings. However, the mounting difficulties of communication with forward commanders, almost all of which now had to be made via London, left him with a very incomplete knowledge of events at the front. This decision was probably correct in view of the dangers of German airpower, but he was to be very much criticized for it later.

In the next two days, May 23 and 24, it became clear that the two-piece north and south pincer attacks on the German scythe, now a bulge over twenty-five miles wide, was less and less likely to succeed, the Allied forces having neither the essential mobility nor the strength to successfully execute the plan. The BEF, short of ammunition, had withdrawn further, and General Blanchard, Billotte's unprepared and confused successor, although still affirming his intention to carry out Weygand's plan, was faced with severe communication problems between his divisions and seemed to have lost control. Reports reaching Weygand were contradictory. French divisions, too, were retreating northward, while Blanchard and Gort were in open disagreement.

Weygand was later to blame himself for not having accepted that the encirclement could not for the moment be broken and that the Allied armies should instead have been concentrated to build a maritime bridgehead, to be supplied by sea and covered by air. Even if the Allies could have agreed on this course of action, the chances of such a bridgehead surviving German airpower would almost certainly have been too slight. To add to Weygand's difficulties, Churchill in London appointed Spears, now a general, as a special liaison officer with Reynaud. Spears and Weygand had met during the First World War and shared a mutual dislike that was later sharpened by Weygand's angry riposte to Spears's review of Foch's memoirs.[5] Spears almost immediately disputed Blanchard's plans and, very disagreeably, the strategy of the air force commander General Vuillemin.

By the evening of May 24 and despite a confident message from Blanchard, Weygand was forced to abandon any remaining hope of a launch of his attack plan. His thoughts now moved to the bridgehead project protecting Boulogne, Calais, and Dunkirk, to be reinforced by fresh troops brought over from England and also some troops withdrawn from Norway—a far from realistic calculation. Gort was now—and in the long term entirely correctly—planning for an evacuation, and the Belgians already appeared to lack initiative. Weygand hoped that the bridgehead would require the Germans to keep substantial forces north of the Somme, thereby easing pressure on the defensive line south of the river. On the 25th he dispatched General Louis Koeltz to try to coordinate the plans of Blanchard, Gort, and the Belgians north of the Somme and sent a special message to the Belgians urging maximum efforts.

The German advance, however, continued to be unstoppable. Boulogne fell on the 25th and Calais after a valiant British defense on the 26th. Worse was to follow on the next day. In the early evening, Weygand was informed that the Belgians were abandoning the fight, exposing the eastern flank of the encircled British and French divisions. The news that the Belgians had decided to give up entirely came as a surprise. Recalling the valor of the Belgian Army in the First World War, Weygand was discouraged and displeased.[6] Military operations in the north declined from attempts to break the German encirclement and turned to the provision of cover for the British evacuation at Dunkirk, which French forces conducted with great resolution, a fact often overlooked in Britain but rightly described by Weygand as a "glorious page." Marching and fighting under continuous air bombardment, five divisions attempted a southeast breakout in vain; out of ammunition, they were obliged to surrender on the 31st. From another five divisions and marine sailors covering the immediate Dunkirk perimeter, 63,000 French soldiers were evacuated to southern

England, the last to leave, on June 4. The remainder became prisoners of war. Weygand could do little apart from putting pressure on the British government to ensure that French troops, too, were to be evacuated and making impassioned pleas for the RAF to provide as much air cover as possible; no other alternative was open for him. He saw the evacuation as no victory but a catastrophe averted.

At an evening meeting of the war council on May 25, a body formed to direct the national effort including President Albert Lebrun, Reynaud, Pétain; the air, navy, and colonial ministers: Weygand, Admiral François Darlan, Vuillemin, and General Jules Buhrer. Weygand first warned that in the event of a further German breakthrough successful resistance would become less and less likely and an armistice would be necessary. Reynaud's immediate reaction was to fight on; he doubted whether Germany would grant an armistice, but both he and the president agreed that Britain should be consulted about the situation. Pétain added a dismissive comment that only ten British divisions were engaged, with none of the national suffering experienced by France, and General Vuillemin sharply criticized the failure of the RAF to supply any effective help. The meeting concluded with the decision that a move of the government from Paris to Bordeaux should be prepared, and Weygand significantly asking what social disorder throughout the country, in particular a communist uprising in Paris, might result from a total destruction of the French Army.[7] The 1789–1871 fault line of deep-seated distrust and fear was widening again. Reynaud agreed to discuss the situation with Churchill the next day and, in particular, again press for increased British air effort, anti-aircraft artillery, and troops.

From the last days of May 1940, Weygand's command responsibility stretched from the Somme to the Swiss border, over three hundred miles. Sixty French divisions remained, many of which were now understrength and short of artillery. Of these divisions only three were armored. Three British divisions, of which one was light armor, also remained or had arrived in the north and were still available. The Germans, able to replace casualties and equipment quickly, could field at least 135 divisions, of which ten were fully armored; these were supported by large numbers of aircraft, in particular dive-bombers, of which France had none.

Weygand records that he saw himself faced by limited options. He considered that a step-by-step strategic defense, an in-depth withdrawal that would oblige the Germans to overcome a series of hill, water, or other defense lines and so wear themselves out in attrition, was now beyond the capability of his forces. To defend a shorter line seemed more realistic. He rejected both any defense of the Paris area and northwest France at the expense of Alsace and Lorraine, Burgundy, and the Rhone (perhaps thereby conceding a German link with the Italian Army) and its alternative, the defense of the old and newly fortified regions, giving up the western seacoast and Paris. With the agreement of General Georges, with whom he conferred daily, he chose a defense on the Aisne-Somme position, the Channel to Reims, with, given fortune, the Maginot Line shielding the northeast. As early as May 26, he had had orders for this strategy approved by the government and issued to forward formations, a decision correct in that the two other alternatives were politically inadmissible. In any event, in military terms, there was no other option. The orders stressed that there could be no retreat, that the fate of the country depended on their execution, and that the defense should be aggressively conducted. In detail he ordered that any German breakthrough must be quickly repulsed by artillery, aircraft, and counterattack; other tactics should be tactical defense in depth by local "hedgehogs" positions, fighting in streets where armor was at a disadvantage, and demolitions. The order was to be read out down the chain of command from major general to ordinary soldiers. It represented a sound military judgment and decision. There was nothing else he could have said or planned; he simply hoped for another September 1914 Marne miracle. The military campaign, however, was already lost. The story of the next sixteen days is one of the realization of this fact by the government, Reynaud, Pétain, and Weygand, and what the loss might represent—the loss of a major campaign or a whole war, the effects of the loss on the people of France, and on the nation's social fabric. First though, there was to be one last battle.

Before an account of the events of the last battle and Weygand's role in it, the stage setting should be illuminated. The roads of northern France were clogged with columns of refugees; conservative estimates place the number of displaced persons at least at 10 million. The properties they had left were being looted. On the roads the elderly often had to be abandoned at local schools, medical centers, or religious foundations. Children were separated from parents. Petty, and sometimes more serious, crime was common. People were exhausted, hungry, and frightened. French soldiers, exhausted after ten more days of very severe fighting, ill-equipped for the ongoing violence of the German air and armored onslaught, had lost whatever confidence they might have had in a French victory. Frontline division commanders complained bitterly that the British were letting them down and that they could not fight on without reinforcement and new equipment. Several thousands of soldiers were German prisoners, unable to communicate with their families. German dive-bombers circled above both refugees and frontline soldiers, preparing their strikes with machine guns or bombs, whose screeching whistle was as terrifying as their fall and explosion. Daily it appeared that Italy was preparing to join the war, which occurred as soon as Mussolini had assured himself that German victory was beyond doubt on June 10. The British had looked after themselves by both evacuating their soldiers and refusing to commit their fighter aircraft force; it would in any case obviously be only be a matter of time before they too were overrun. Cities, including Paris, were soon going to fall to the Germans, and the government itself was planning to flee south to Bordeaux. Neither 1914 nor even 1870 had seen anything like it. Weygand himself received a message that his son Jacques had been captured by the Germans, only to receive a little later a telephone message from him at the front.

It was against this darkening background, the 1st Army Group with its elite units reduced to remnants, that Weygand first sought to build his second Channel to Somme/Aisne to Maginot Line front with a battle cry of "Activity, Solidarity, Resolution." On May 27, he called for an offensive strike at the enemy with the priority of "direction" across their line of advance so as to throw the attackers off course. If the Germans again broke through the "fragments" of surviving formations, any units were to form centers of resistance and fight on for the sake of honor. At this time these orders appeared to reflect the best that could be done, but very soon they became unrealistic. Even more unreal was the desperate hope of aid from the United States.

At daily meetings and conferences with Reynaud and Pétain, Weygand repeated that the cause of France's misfortune was the prewar failure to

prepare for the war. He continued to press for British support and experience, and voiced his anxiety over the likely inability of France to resist a
breakthrough. By the 29th his thoughts had moved to the possibility of es-
tablishing a last-ditch bastion in Brittany and the transporting of the last
two classes of reservists to North Africa to prepare to continue the fight.
The difficulties very quickly appeared insuperable. The preparation of a
solid redoubt was beyond French resources that could be mustered in the
time available, the transport of 500,000 men to North Africa was impossible to arrange, and in any case there were no facilities in North Africa
prepared to receive, arm, and train them. Further, Weygand was becoming
even more concerned that Italy and perhaps even also Spain might join
the Germans. Britain, it appeared, could not provide many more troops
before late June and was not prepared to offer more air support, Churchill
adding that he now had to face a possible invasion threat.

On the ground, Weygand completed his preparations for defense. In the
west the 3rd Army Group of the Sixth Army and a hurriedly reconstituted
Seventh Army under General Antoine Besson would cover Paris, while
on the east General André-Gaston Prételat's 2nd Army Group of Eighth,
Fifth, Fourth, Third, and Second Armies would protect the northeast,
with certain towns marked out for special fortified defense areas. Prételat
would have preferred to conduct a defense in depth withdrawal, but Weygand forbade this and moved one of his Armies, the Fourth, to the west
on the Lower Seine. In these last days of May, the German ground forces
were regrouping following their earlier victories; intelligence reaching
Weygand indicated that troop movements warned of two likely areas
of attack—the more dangerous through Amiens targeting the Lower
Seine and a second further east through country suitable for tanks in
Champagne. Weygand accordingly created a new 4th Army Group made
up of two armies taken from the 2nd Group, the Fourth and Second Armies, together with a hurriedly formed Tenth Army under the command
of Huntziger. That left the remainder of the 2nd Group to hold the fortified
zones of the northeast. Two British divisions, one very hurriedly assembled armored division, and an older infantry division were the most that
the United Kingdom could contribute, but Weygand hoped that he would
soon be able to reinforce both army groups with French reinforcements
from North Africa and elsewhere.

Weygand assessed that the most dangerous of the threats now posed by the Germans was the exploitation of the five bridgehead crossings of the Somme that they had achieved earlier. A series of French attacks seeking to clear the river's southern bank, while gaining some local successes including a well-earned local victory led by Colonel de Gaulle, failed to remove the Germans. To further strengthen French defenses, division generals were ordered to construct solid roadblocks at crossroads and villages, to institute a system of observers to provide intelligence and prevent false alarms, and to use the few French aircraft available to strike the Germans armor while it was regrouping. For the defense of Paris, Weygand set out specific instructions for defense against a sudden German armored assault or raid and against "fifth column" activities; these latter were not clearly defined, but the antiwar Left were considered obvious suspects. A series of advance positions along the Seine, the Lower Oise, and Lower Ourcq to Château-Thierry on the Marne were hastily prepared; further works east and south were planned, but little was accomplished before they were overtaken by events. Allegations, never substantiated, later claimed that some formation commanders held back the building of these defenses in order to facilitate a German victory, a soldier-to-soldier just peace, and the installation of a right-wing government.

During this period Weygand, still full of energy, continued to visit General Georges daily, maintained good communications with Besson, and held two meetings with Prételat. He recorded that he had absolute confidence in the abilities of the different army commanders, most of whom he knew personally, but all raised the same complaint—why was there no air cover; did the government not understand the gravity of the situation? Weygand had also to give a daily briefing to the prime minister and to the deputy prime minister, the increasingly cold and depressed Pétain, with whom nevertheless he worked in accord. Weygand's command decisions were eminently sensible; nothing more could have been done in the circumstances. Whether a different, more personal frontline general-to-soldier style of command would have provided greater motivation is very doubtful. In any case Weygand could have visited only a small number of units. Correctly assessing a renewed German onslaught, he prepared a new urgent and emotive appeal to his forces on June 4, beginning by saying that the Battle of France had begun and ending that the fate of the country depended on their tenacity. The order went out on the 5th, the day the German assault opened.

The next ten days were of such importance in the history of the Second World War, in the history of France, and in the life of Weygand that a day-by-day account is necessary.

The German assault plan provided for two massive attacks. The first, to open on the 5th, was to be undertaken by four armies and three mechanized corps, each consisting of two armored and two motorized divisions, to be mounted from the captured Somme bridgeheads and tasked to attack on both sides of Paris, as Weygand had foreseen. The second attack, to open on the 9th, would employ three armies and four mechanized corps, each consisting of two armored and two motorized corps tasked to cross the Aisne between Soissons and Reims and then swing east toward Alsace. The French 3rd Army Group was able to contain the German tank and infantry divisions on the first day, with no key positions lost though the menace of the tanks remained. On the same day Weygand received reports from the French military attaché in Rome that Italy was about to enter the war, but this declaration would not be followed by a major offensive in the Alps nor attacks on Corsica or Tunisia. The attaché gave no reason for the decision not to attack, but after the costs and losses suffered by the Italians in Spain and Abyssinia, Italy's army was in poor shape for further combat.[8] Weygand nevertheless took precautions.

The next two days were ones of ever-mounting concern. Although one German tank attack had been brought to a halt following effective strikes by French aircraft, on June 6 German columns made advances on each flank of their Somme attack. The prepositioned French defensive areas fought well, but in the absence of reserves or other units to relieve them they were overcome. On the 7th Weygand felt compelled to order a general withdrawal of 2nd Army Group extending from the Lower Seine, the approaches to Paris, the Ourcq, and the Marne. The withdrawal had to be made in the midst of the chaos caused by fleeing refugees and methodical German bombing (which on a visit to the front Weygand experienced for himself). The Seine bridges had to be prepared for destruction.

June 8 opened with a bad tactical decision by the Tenth Army on the extreme left flank, an error of judgment by local command and one that led to the army being split in two. The IX Corps, including a British division, were driven toward the coast, the rest of the Tenth Army eastward, resulting in the opening of a gap opening between the two. Weygand immediately reorganized the command structure, but the damage had been done. Extrication of the IX Corps became impossible. Formations broken from contact with those on their flank, including the British 51st Highland Division, were forced to surrender on June 11 and 12. Elsewhere the line held at enormous cost in casualties. Among Weygand's visitors at the time was Charles de Gaulle, newly promoted to the rank of *général de brigade* and recently appointed an undersecretary by Reynaud. In fact de Gaulle was quietly advising Reynaud to replace Weygand by Huntziger, but Reynaud said that Pétain would never agree.

The two days that followed, June 9–10, were to show that the issue was now one of national honor more than any hope of resistance and ultimate success. On the 9th the second German assault was launched on the 4th Army Group front. Weygand issued a dramatic appeal to all, ending with "We have come to the last quarter of an hour. Stand firm." The Germans had reached the approaches to Paris. All reserves available for the front had been committed; North Africans and other reserves from the Alps were being re-formed in the south and were not yet available. Totally exhausted, the men at the front were forced to intermingle on the overcrowded roads with columns of refugees who had no food, water, or shelter. Many soldiers lost all incentive to continue fighting.

Italy entered the war on June 10, but its army's attempts to invade France were repulsed with little difficulty.

As the situation worsened, with German troops beginning to cross the Seine and threatening a breakthrough in Champagne, the French government left Paris for Tours, Weygand having pointed out that the old forts surrounding the capital were of no value. He too had to move his headquarters from Montry to Briare near Orléans further south; the headquarters of Georges and Doumenc also moved closer to Briare.

On the evening of the 11th, Weygand gave the prime minister a very clear and realistic written appreciation of the situation. He warned that the situation in the Paris region and Champagne was desperate and that a collapse of French resistance was almost inevitable. He did not at this point advocate or even mention an armistice, but he felt that Reynaud, still talking of a Breton redoubt, seemed incapable of grasping the mortal dangers and was living in a different world. In turn Reynaud, himself confused and overburdened, sent de Gaulle to Orléans to ask General Huntziger if he would be willing to succeed Weygand as commander in chief. Huntziger agreed, but Reynaud subsequently changed his mind.[9]

Weygand prepared new orders for a general withdrawal. The 2nd Army Group would move toward Sarrebourg, the Fourth toward Châlons-sur-Marne, Troyes, and Nevers with Rouen, Argentan, and Orléans on list, with a view to holding a line across the center of France from Caen, Tours, Saumur, the middle Loire, Clamecy, and Dijon to the Doubs forests. Rearguard actions were to be fought. On his own initiative and with the thought of both the people and the unique beauty of Paris, Weygand also issued a preparatory order for the declaration of Paris as an open city and therefore that no roads or bridges were to be destroyed. During the day he told the prime minister of this decision. Reynaud neither agreed nor disagreed, and the order was confirmed and issued the following day, June 12. General Georges was in full agreement with the decision.

Churchill and Anthony Eden, his foreign secretary, were fully briefed at a meeting that same evening, but they continued to resist all pleas for the full commitment of the Royal Air Force. The atmosphere of the meeting was friendly but melancholy. Churchill expressed his full confidence in Weygand, his great admiration for the French Army, and his sincere regret that the United Kingdom could do little more to help. But Churchill did affirm that whatever happened, Britain would continue the war. Reynaud concluded the meeting by firmly asserting that, ultimately, any decision on whether to continue the war was a political one for the government, a very clear instruction. Weygand testily replied that he would be happy to serve under anyone who could provide a way of escaping from the consequences of their present reality.

By the morning of the 12th, the Germans were advancing steadily on most sections, creating serious new dangers as French formations increasingly lost contact with those on their flanks. The coordinated line then unraveled. Briefings to government ministers that particular armies, corps, and divisions were still in action became more and more unreal, as Weygand knew too well. To add to Weygand's difficulties, de Gaulle reappeared. As before, he was overtly polite to Weygand but intent on promoting ideas of his own: being given command of France's remaining

1,200 tanks; a defense of southern Brittany; and, if necessary, fighting in the streets of Paris, all to the resentment of Weygand.

With only bad news continuing to arrive from the front, at 7:34 A M on the next day, June 13, Weygand decided to ask the Supreme War Council, meeting with Churchill in attendance, to arrange for an armistice. He conceived this as an arrangement totally distinct from a Dutch-style capitulation, which would mean a total surrender and collapse, weapons and equipment abandoned, the Germans free to go anywhere, a national disgrace. Capitulation was also a grave military offense; in 1873 Marshal Bazaine had been sentenced to death (commuted to twenty years' imprisonment) for surrendering his besieged army to the Prussians, thereby precipitating France's defeat.[10] The Germans would be free to reach the Mediterranean coast in two or three days, preventing any hope of withdrawing troops to North Africa, and even worse would be free to use bases in Italy or Franco's Spain to fly troops to North Africa. The Norway campaign had highlighted the Germans' ability to fly soldiers by air, and in North Africa the French garrison forces were in no state to provide any effective defense.

An armistice, as Weygand saw it at the time, would be an agreed negotiated ceasefire; armies would remain where they were. The Army of France would be shown to have kept its honor by its valiant defense of the nation over the last three weeks, and no more of the thousands of French soldiers in action would have to lay down their lives. Since May 10, the French Army had lost at least 60,000 men killed (of which about one-quarter were African colonials), 150,000 wounded, and 1,500,000 prisoners or missing—precise figures were and remain impossible to collect. With an armistice time would be gained, and in the breathing space, fresh allies, in particular the United States, might rally to the cause and the conflict be resumed in better times.

For Weygand there were of course the other local factors: his dislike and contempt for Reynaud and the evil influence of his mistress, the Comtesse de Portes, who had just been killed in a motor car crash; his disgust at the lifestyle and sexual behavior at a time of crisis of various other members of the government; and his belief that neither the March 28th agreement with Britain by which both countries agreed not to conclude a separate peace (an agreement planned for the contingency of an

Allied victory) nor the reorganization of the Council of Ministers, which included de Gaulle, was necessarily legally binding as they had not been approved by the legislature. He also said that he thought the government should remain in Paris, accepting the likelihood of capture, a suggestion that he later admitted to have been a mistake.

A misunderstanding, hardly surprising in the chaotic conditions of the time, arose on June 14. The British Army General Sir Alan Brooke was said to have advised London that Weygand had told him that French resistance had ceased and therefore any further British involvement in France should cease. Earlier that day Weygand had included British troops along with the movement of French formations at a meeting at which Brooke had been present. The misunderstanding was cleared up on a personal basis, but thereafter Weygand declared that he was no longer responsible for British formations.

It is said that on one occasion Weygand was heard to murmur, "Who am I to order the deaths of many hundreds more Frenchmen when I am not even sure that I am one myself," but the evidence for this is uncertain, and it did not affect his judgment. What is certain, however, is that defeat and capitulation were to strike at the core pillars of Weygand's lifetime values and philosophy—his Catholic faith and the French Army. No very seriously practicing Christian could fail to be moved by the suffering of millions on the roads; no general responsible for the lives of his men and the honor of his army and country could possibly approve the capitulation favored by some of the political leaders, soon to include Reynaud. Weygand argued his case with increasing intemperance over the next ten days, making bitter and lasting enemies by his shouting, and later, outright disobedience. But he did not engage in any form of political plotting.

The decision to request an armistice was a bitter one for Weygand, but there is no question that his judgment was entirely correct. French North Africa under attack by the Italians from Libya and the Germans flown in by air could not have been secured even if capitulation had not involved the French Navy. Weygand himself had not envisaged that an armistice would lead, shortly afterward, to the collapse of the Third Republic for which he had had little regard but to which he had affirmed loyalty. He refused to leave France, as Reynaud hoped to do, he refused to preside over a capitulation if he was ordered to do so, and he refused to resign. Later, he simply believed Reynaud had abdicated responsibility. He saw himself as a victim of duty, faced with a situation he had foreseen ten years earlier. Now called upon to be the guardian of army and nation, he said he would willingly have accepted death if he believed it would have been of any use. Others saw crude, personal ambition—for what they did not make clear—and called for his dismissal.

When a few days later the armistice was agreed to, the logic of Weygand's argument was confirmed. It spared some 2 million or more French soldiers from death or captivity in Germany, others from mutiny, and as Weygand saw it at the time, prevented the immediate pillaging of France's resources in agriculture and industry and German military administration over all of France, followed by the deportation of civilians. The navy did not have to be surrendered, the colonies were left alone, and Mussolini's ambitions left in check. In terms of immediate interest France appeared to have escaped lightly; no intelligence available at the time suggested otherwise. France was not to be Poland yet. Disenchantment with Britain was complete. No one had any idea of Hitler's maturing long-term plans for France as a food and energy supply colony and as a pool of cheap labor, or his plans for the systematic destruction of "decadent" French culture. The German armistice terms, carefully prepared on a German agenda, were not thought ungenerous, as a British collapse would surely soon follow. A rump French army would be left to secure areas not under German occupation, while planning went forward for continuing the war against Britain.

Meanwhile, the Germans were advancing fast, approaching Chartres and Romilly-sur-Seine; there were rumors, later to be shown as false, of a German-supported communist uprising in Paris. Frontline generals with whom Weygand spoke pleaded for a cessation of hostilities. A meeting with the Council of Ministers only added to the confusion. As Weygand set out the military situation, Reynaud, backed by de Gaulle, continued to argue for a Breton redoubt. His critics claimed then and later that Weygand had painted an unnecessarily gloomy picture and tried to strengthen his case by commenting that the army seemed unwilling to fight on. In fact, the reality was gloomy enough and others supported Weygand's view, saying that he was brave enough to face the facts.

Weygand stated that he would not agree to an armistice that involved the surrender of a single French warship. Reynaud spoke of a Dutch-style government in exile after a capitulation, to which Weygand testily replied that three years in safety and comfort was a rather different fate from that of the soldiers who would be left behind, adding that he himself would never leave France. This reply would later be criticized as an act of open disobedience, although it was better seen as an expression of Weygand's loyalty to his soldiers. Weygand then abruptly left the meeting. It nevertheless continued. Pétain, who up to this point had said little, offered his opinions, delivering them in an ex cathedra style. To Reynaud's intense annoyance, he argued fiercely for an armistice and for the government to remain in France. The only decision reached at the meeting was that the government must move to Bordeaux, for which Pétain requested "open city" status be sought from the Germans.

Much of the night and the next day, June 14, during a sixteen-hour train journey to Bordeaux, Weygand spent considering advice in a letter from Pétain. The day was to see the German entry and occupation of Paris, with all that it signified. On his arrival in Bordeaux on the 15th, after a motor accident in which Weygand was bruised, Pétain and others urged him to restrain from emotive and ill-tempered language. At a meeting with Reynaud alone Weygand again requested an armistice while Reynaud continued to talk of Brittany; there was no agreement but neither was there violent disagreement. That, however, was to follow after a Council of Ministers meeting from which he and Admiral Darlan had both been specifically excluded and told to wait in an adjoining room. In the meeting a proposal for an armistice was put forward by a former prime minister, Chautemps, who suggested that an acceptable armistice should be brokered by a neutral country, which could then pressure Britain to acquiesce. Reynaud disagreed, but the council voted to present the proposal to London first. This decision led Reynaud to an unwise desire to assert his authority as prime minister.

After the meeting had ended, Reynaud summoned Weygand and told him that in accord with the meeting he was to capitulate, adding, which was not the case, that the council had approved capitulation. Weygand stepped back and in a charged voice retorted that nothing on earth would make him execute such an order to an army that had fought so well, and that any suggestion he had so agreed was false. Furious, he added that the entire army would be made prisoner and that even if he were to be disgraced and shot he would not capitulate and he had had enough of such talk. He would return to his command, await further orders, but not obey the one he had just been given. Reynaud, frightened, exhausted, and shaken, replied that after all it had only been an idea and the general should keep calm, a reply that only increased Weygand's anger and led him to accuse Reynaud of lying and of summoning him from Lebanon to be a "yes man." Reynaud then broke off the conversation. Still in a white-hot rage, Weygand demanded to see President Lebrun, who agreed to meet him but only in Reynaud's presence. Weygand asked Lebrun whether it had been simply to ambush him that he had been brought back from Beirut to carry the responsibility for the situation. When Lebrun replied that his behavior was unconstitutional, Weygand returned to the charge, shouting that when in the 1930 he had asked to see President Lebrun to protest against reductions in the army he had been told that this, too, was unconstitutional. In slightly more moderate language, he turned to Reynaud and said that he would now accept only written orders from him. He would never capitulate, and if the government did not ask for an armistice he would fight on to the end. He then departed on his way to meet with Pétain, who as deputy prime minister had been at the session of the council. Pétain said that the council had not agreed on a capitulation, but that he himself was very tired and might not have heard everything.

Weygand returned to his headquarters, expecting an order of dismissal, possibly even arrest. In fact, Reynaud directed that Weygand be arrested, and one of his ministers, Mandel, even demanded it, but no such orders were executed. Neither did Weygand receive any policy or strategic guidance. Indecision remained.

The generalissimo of the French and Allied Armies had now committed a second act of disobedience, this time a gross and flagrant refusal of orders given by his country's president and prime minister, even if the orders may not have been properly authorized. How serious was this act of disobedience? Was it simply a personality clash between Weygand and Reynaud; a major breach in the Republic order of civil-military relations; or the tragic culmination of ten years of bitter controversy over policy and strategy? Whatever the rights and wrongs of this particular act, Weygand was not alone among military men who had become so embittered that they had turned to an increasingly authoritarian mindset, asserting military power over civilian. They began to see their actions as justified in the name of the army and the nation in a confrontation with those they considered directly responsible for the plight of France, politicians who now appeared willing to depart into hospitable exile and leave the military to bear the consequences and the blame. Weygand himself later urged (not very convincingly) that he had not violated the traditional order placing civilian over military power. He had merely said that given a certain order he would resign, but that it was in fact the civilian government, not he, that ought to resign. But viewed historically all of this was in reality only stage setting; the script for the play had been written elsewhere 150 years earlier, and Weygand, Reynaud, and others were just the latest actors playing their assigned roles.

June 16, 1940, opened with a communication from President Roosevelt making it clear that the United States was not going to intervene. At the council's morning meeting Pétain, still deputy prime minister, read out a letter of resignation saying that there must be an immediate ceasefire. He was persuaded to hold his hand until the British government had replied to the Chautemps proposal. Before this official reply had been processed, de Gaulle telephoned from London with news of a project for an Anglo-French national union. Reynaud was enthusiastic, but the majority present saw the offer as a British plot to take control over France. Weygand also opposed the project, arguing that in its current state of weakness, France would become a British client state. The debate was stormy, and in the course of it or shortly afterward, Reynaud resigned, advising President Lebrun to appoint Pétain in his place. The latter, it seemed, had been awaiting such a summons with a prepared list of ministers. He was to be the last prime minister of the Third Republic and was to use his position to destroy it.

The most significant opponent of these events was de Gaulle, who, fearing arrest by Weygand, had departed for London with the help of Spears. In his historic June 18 broadcast he proclaimed that the fight must continue. France had lost a battle but not the war. In his opposition, at first not thought very significant except by a small minority, de Gaulle opened a vendetta, to become increasingly bitter, between himself and Weygand—and of course Pétain. However, de Gaulle was in London, not in command of troops or having to face the terrifying and tragic consequences of his country's catastrophe at first hand.

6

MINISTER FOR NATIONAL DEFENSE
JUNE–SEPTEMBER 1940

Among the new ministers, Weygand was to be minister for national defense, with Huntziger as minister for war.[1] Most of the other ministers, however, reflected the policy aims of Marshal Philippe Pétain, now eighty-four years old, the hero of Verdun, the general who had restored the morale, discipline, and self-respect of the French Army after the "mutinies" of 1917, the only one of the First World War marshals still on his feet, but a man whose mental clarity of vision and analysis was already noted by observers as declining during the course of the day.[2] He was no friend of Great Britain; in the bitterness of defeat he saw Britain as simply trying to use France to suit British needs. He had been much influenced by the Spanish Civil War, which confirmed his belief that social order and some form of firm moral regeneration were needed in France. The pattern for this was to be that of the new national slogan, *Travail, Famille, Patrie.* Youth organizations and schools would be restructured along very authoritarian lines, as would labor and agriculture. These changes would take shape later in the institutions of the "National Revolution," the semimilitary youth organization Chantiers de la Jeunesse, the Secours National, the Corporation Paysanne, and the Légion Française des Combattants, and in institutionalized anti-Semitism.

In his own words Pétain saw himself as making a supreme self-sacrifice—the gift of his person to the nation. Other political activity that was not supportive of the new regime was divisive and must cease. For a nation suffering something resembling post-traumatic stress disorder following the military defeat, the Marshal appeared to be and presented himself as the savior of the nation, who soldier to soldier had gained an acceptable deal from the Germans. A huge, almost hysterical national popularity cult developed around Pétain and was to last, despite some disenchantment, until the arrival of de Gaulle on French soil in 1944. In June 1940, however, Pétain was receiving some 2,000 laudatory letters every day.

Looking ahead, the tragedy of this fast-aging man, surrounded by fascist and quasi-fascist advisers, was to be a downward path: reluctant concessions to the Germans; anti-Semitic discrimination, with later deportation of French Jews, including children, to extermination camps; and a brutal fascist militia. The later brutality and compromises with the Germans by the ministers of his regime were not clear to foresee in June 1940. It was later that the savior of France was to become the national disgrace, to end his days in prison in ignominy and shame, largely through his own self-importance and delusions of omniscience.

For Weygand, and despite an up-and-down relationship over the years, Pétain was a Marshal of France, the nation's highest honor, awarded only by a vote in the legislature, and an honor that could never be taken away. For a man whose whole life had been built around the military ethos of discipline and obedience, Weygand believed that even a full general, as he was, should serve a Marshal. Differing viewpoints could be put to him, cooperation with some of his advisers could be circumvented or ignored, but ultimately the authority of a Marshal was essential for military and social cohesion, particularly in the chaos of the summer of 1940. For Weygand, there was no question whatever about the legitimacy of the new regime as the lawful government of France. As such it was of course fully recognized by the United States and other foreign governments.

Weygand realized that chances of any international support were small, despite emotional appeals. He believed that at some time the United States must enter the war but that the time was not yet, and in any case help would take time to arrive. Great Britain could probably look after itself but could not help France, and Stalin's Soviet Union was a German ally. Resentment against Britain's withdrawal of troops and failure to provide air support would only intensify after the Royal Navy's attack on the French fleet at Mers el-Kébir on July 4. Weygand's support of the British had turned to dislike and distrust, but he still held out hope for an ultimate victory, British-led or including Britain as an ally. He also hoped that the armistice would secure an early release of the thousands of prisoners of war held by the Germans and that Italian ambitions in North Africa would be curbed, as Hitler, for his own reasons, was to do.

For first time in many years Weygand was now briefly in general accord with the government and an actual member of its "Small Council" inner circle. Weygand knew that as a minister he might disapprove of actions by other ministers, but he would have to support them or go. De Gaulle was still seen as a very junior, recently promoted general who at a very difficult time was being disobedient, arrogating power (he had issued his own orders to troops in southern Brittany) and authority for himself to which he was in no way entitled. Weygand agreed to remain commander in chief in addition to his ministerial responsibilities after the cessation of fighting.

The new government acted quickly. The Spanish government was asked to request that Germany cease combat operations immediately and set out peace terms. Pétain made his "gift of his person" broadcast to a wildly enthusiastic nation, but an ill-judged phrase in it, "il faut cesser le combat," was interpreted by many regiments and individual soldiers as meaning that it was imperative to stop fighting. Weygand had to issue an urgent order that fighting must continue until an armistice had been agreed and signed, but this order came too late in many cases. The version of Pétain's address printed in newspapers amended the phrase to read "il faut tenter de cesser le combat," "it is essential to try to end the fighting."

The German advance continued as they wanted the strongest hand in any negotiations. Within the new cabinet France's neo-fascists' creeping entry into ministerial office began. Those known to favor some form of limitation of German power predicated on President Lebrun and others leaving for Africa were thwarted. Weygand used all his influence on Pétain to prevent the appointment of Pierre Laval, the arch advocate of collaboration with the Germans, as foreign minister. But further political changes in favor of collaboration were to follow before long, with Laval featuring as the most likely heir to Pétain. The government itself first moved to Clermont-Ferrand, outside the zone to be occupied by the Germans, for two days and then on July 1 to Vichy with its many comfortable but largely unoccupied hotels. There Weygand was to remain, in his short spell as minister for national defense, until September 5.

His first ministerial act, early in the morning of June 17, was to accede to an urgent request from the British ambassador that the arrangement made by France for the production and delivery of over a thousand aircraft—fighters, medium bombers, dive-bombers, and reconnaissance planes—together with spare motors and equipment, being made under contract in the United States, be transferred to Britain. Over five hundred of the aircraft were already built—to the profit and much needed revival of American industry and eventual help to the British in North Africa. The contract had been opposed by the American air corps generals and also by the national hero figure Colonel Charles Lindbergh, who hated anything to do with Britain. Weygand instantly agreed, but with discretion did not openly publicize his decision for three months. He also quietly arranged for France's supply of "heavy water" and two nuclear scientists to be sent to Britain. The move of the French stock of uranium to Britain proved too difficult; it was instead sent to and concealed in Morocco, unknown to the Germans. Weygand also agreed to the departure of the French fleet from Toulon and elsewhere to ports in North Africa, home ports being under threat of air attack.

Also on June 17, Weygand agreed to declare Lyon, like Paris, open, after an impassioned plea from Herriot for his native city. On the next day Weygand had to issue a further order to the army to fight on until an armistice had been agreed upon. Early on the morning of the 19th the Spanish government indicated that the Germans were now prepared to set out their conditions for an armistice. It appeared that they would not request the surrender of French warships to the Germans, the one condition that Pétain would not have countenanced. At the Council of Ministers it was agreed that the French delegation should be headed not by Weygand but by Huntziger, the idea being apparently to keep Weygand as some kind of reserve, though it fell to Weygand to tell Huntziger of his selection for the miserable task.

Charles-Léon Huntziger was *Coloniale* officer who had earned a reputation for negotiating skills in Syria before extending it to the battlefield. He and a supporting team of staff officers and officials were sent off to the same railway carriage in Compiègne that had been the scene of France's triumph in November 1918, and there were subjected to a number of humiliations. The government itself was still in administrative confusion, uncertain as to whether the German army might not suddenly appear on its doorstep. Some German units had already crossed the Loire, and the Maginot Line was outflanked.

On June 21 Weygand received his first news from Huntziger at Compiègne. The Germans allowed him no liaison staff, and all messages had to be *en clair*. The main conditions, almost immediately accepted, are well-known: German occupation of all of the north, including Paris, and all the Atlantic Coast; reduction of the French Army to 100,000 men; the disarming of all combat aircraft; and the surrender of all Germans opposed to Hitler who had taken refuge in France. There was to be no release of French Army prisoners held by the Germans, only a vague promise that their living conditions would be improved. No surrender of colonies was demanded; that Hitler did not immediately demand air and naval facilities in French North Africa was one of his major strategic errors in the war. Further, the French were to be allowed a military force in North Africa, which they claimed necessary in case of a nationalist uprising or a British invasion. This force was later to be of very great importance.

Above all there was in the vital issue of the French Navy. There was no demand for the surrender of ships, only that they should be disarmed and proceed to an agreed port; later North African ports were accepted for this purpose. Huntziger's efforts to have Paris excluded from the German occupied zone were a failure. After a separate but almost identical agreement with the Italians, hostilities finally ended at 00:35 on June 25, 1940.

Hitler made substantial gains from these terms. There could still be a French government responsible for day-to-day administration of France; he did not have to create a military government distracting him from plans to invade Britain. Essential for French respect, there could still be a French professional army—not a civilian national guard. Against the advice of his sailors, Hitler was not particularly concerned with the French Navy so long as the ships could not be used by the British. Deliberately, discussion of an eventual peace treaty had been ruled out by the Germans. Later it appeared that Hitler would ideally have liked to take Pétain and Weygand into custody, but by not doing so and with the apparent moderation of the terms, he strengthened the voices of those surrounding Pétain to end the British alliance and strike a new relationship with Germany. More stringent terms could follow when Germany had defeated Britain.

For the French, contemporary and most subsequent perceptions have held that Weygand's views and actions were in the national best interest, that honor had been preserved. The colonies, in particular the North African territories, were secured, which was a very real gain as Great Britain was in no position to prevent a German airborne invasion. And most important of all, the navy's ships were saved from humiliating surrender. (In fairness to Admiral Darlan and the honor of the French Navy, if they had been ordered to surrender they would have either fled to a safe refuge or blown up the ships). The Germans also conceded an undertaking not to use French aircraft against the British. It was the view of many, including Weygand himself, that the armistice was the least dishonorable option for the nation and the least wretched for France's distracted and suffering civilian population possible. A separate armistice, conceding only the town of Menton and two very small regions of southeast France to Italian occupation, was agreed upon a little later; the Italian Army invasion had been held in firm check. Much later, after the end of the war, it was alleged that at the time Weygand had boosted his argument for the armistice by asserting that Great Britain would not fight for long. There is no certain evidence for this; more likely is that in order to press his case he might have made a carefully nuanced expression of doubt. Certainly he continued to see the armistice primarily as a truce. His immediate concerns at the time were containing General Charles Noguès and many other officers in North Africa from continuing to preach ongoing war with no understanding of events in France and with no resources, and General Georges Catroux in the same state of ignorance in Indochina from surrendering to the Japanese. In this context the actions of de Gaulle in London calling for continued fighting did not seem of priority importance; instead his views appeared disloyal, unrealistic, and only likely to lead to more German demands. With the fall of Reynaud, de Gaulle was no longer a minister. He was ordered to report back for reappointment, an order that he ignored.

Weygand spent much of his time away from his office in Vichy's Hôtel Thermal. He issued an order of the day thanking his men for their bravery and service, adding the interesting clause "your task is not ended." He visited generals and regiments to thank the men personally for their efforts, congratulating many and awarding decorations and medals, all duties that he found very emotional. Especially difficult were the Maginot Line garrisons under General Charles Condé, who asserted that they had not been defeated. They only agreed to cease hostilities if the Germans immediately withdrew from a number of cities, including Lyon, south of the demarcation line. This withdrawal was in fact in progress at the time, but the garrisons were denied the honors of war by the Germans.

At the political level, the next few weeks were ones of confusion and division. There were those who saw Pétain as a 1940 equivalent of Thiers in the 1870s, restoring political order out of chaos; others saw the future of France as a corporate state, along the lines of Portugal rather than the showy fascism of Italy. Many, probably including the majority of the general public, wanted change with the departure of the 1930s political generation but were not clear or in agreement on what a new generation should do—whether, for example, the Third Republic should continue or be replaced, and if so by what.

It would seem that Weygand himself was far from clear in his own mind on the wider issues. In some woolly thinking, an exaggerated product of his perception and experience of the previous fifteen years, he wrote a memorandum setting out his views of France's plight, the evils of Freemasonry, class hatred, political compromise dealers, capitalists, and malign international influences, with the need to excise them for the future. Rather surprisingly he also argued against the heavy use of North African troops in defense of the *métropole,* saying France should be defended by Frenchmen, a long-term consequence of his 1930s opposition to reductions in the draft. He was even doubtful of the worth of men who had recently become naturalized Frenchmen. The situation in France, then, only confirmed the views that he had expressed in the 1930s as to the general weak moral state of the nation, in particular concerning schools and youth. On the other hand, no firm evidence exists that he wanted an end to the Third Republic as a constitution with its weak executive. He was also quite clear in his opposition to any form of a one-party state and played a lead role in blocking the concept. He also tried, without success, to block a proposal that there should be trials for those perceived to have been responsible for France's defeat, saying such trials would be divisive at a time when national unity was essential.

Many, including cultural figures such as André Gide together with most of the right-wing writers of the 1930s, were now willing to see the end of the Republic, some regarding its demise as an act of expiation necessary to perform for the sake of future generations. The end followed on July 9, when the senate voted for constitutional reform, and on the next day, when members of both chambers of the legislature sitting together voted for the grant of total power to Marshal Pétain, including the preparation of a constitution for a lay *Etat Français,* a new "French State." Pétain's view of a state based on a social hierarchy founded on a romantic nostalgia for peasant values of work, with community replacing individualism, was becoming daily more clear.

For Weygand himself the state remained lay, permitting measures of tolerance. There was reassurance of its propriety to be found in his own respect for the authority of Pétain as a Marshal and the support given by Catholic bishops and ministers together with other Christian denominations, while opposition came from only a small number of socialists and radicals. His belief that the *Etat Français* could become an influence for good was to prove a very serious error of judgment, and here, where there is no direct military issue, it can be argued that Weygand had allowed his mind to be conditioned toward authority.

At the time, however, Weygand continued to see himself more as a military counselor or expert adviser than as a political advisor or constitutional reformer, tasked to coordinate the work of three individual service ministers. It was in wider political fields that he almost at once found himself marching out of step with others in the government, in particular Laval, now deputy prime minister. These men saw the armistice as a period in which the Germans could be converted from being enemies to being supporters by the French authorities' ignoring certain German illegal activities while making concessions and collaborating with the now very different Europe. Weygand's views were precisely the reverse; the armistice provided a truce within which covert preparation for a return to combat with Germany must be the priority. In the midst was Pétain, convinced that the Germans would win the war and that collaboration was therefore prudent and inescapable, but who throughout the few months in which he retained real power consistently forbade any military action against Britain.

Within the Laval camp there was submissive acceptance and toleration of the de facto if not yet de jure annexation of Alsace and Lorraine, the denial of free movement between northern France and Belgium, and the Germans' deliberate pillaging of factories, farms, libraries, research institutes, museums, and private homes. Weygand sought open radio broadcasts demanding restitution for these actions, which were all breaches of the armistice. The Pétain government sanctioned only written notes; these of course the Germans ignored. For Weygand, who had no illusions about the Germans and believed that they best understood only very firm resolution, the armistice policy ought to have been to challenge the Germans when they committed these acts, particularly the military occupation of the Channel ports.

Weygand concerned himself with the preparation for the Armistice Army, reduced in size but still in his view the "Soul of the Nation," 100,000 strong, planned to be of eight small divisions, each of three infantry brigades of two regiments, a light artillery, possibly an anti-aircraft brigade, and a *horsed* mobile brigade, because the Germans had banned any motorized vehicles and tanks. Covertly Weygand worked for this army's future efficiency with measures that included concealed preparations for an additional 200,000 men, the hiding of equipment and stores for future use, especially weapons not too difficult to conceal such as machine guns and mortars, and instigation of a cover system of "armistice leave" by which he could quietly retain a number of officers over and above the 100,000 army establishment. Regimental colors, traditions, and music were to be maintained. There were to be no more African troops in France.

Weygand also secured the return from the Occupied Zone, often difficult in the chaotic transport conditions of the time, of officers whom he wanted to brief on his views on the role of the much-reduced army, and also the return of wounded soldiers. He covered the move of the Service de Renseignements (SR), the main French military intelligence service, to Unoccupied France and also, to a safe chateau in the south, the French and Polish cypher experts. France's two Enigma machines were sent to Morocco for safekeeping. Weygand also sponsored the creation of a new secret intelligence service, the Bureau des Menées Antinationales (antinational activities) to collect intelligence on Axis military movements and activities. The bureau was to provide valuable material in the months that followed.³ The service of expert munitions and engineering experts was retained, often under nonmilitary guise. Although Weygand successfully carried out these activities, the Germans and those who sought collaboration were suspicious of him, his vigorous protests undermining his own position. Most French Army officers bowed to national necessity and loyalty to Pétain and Weygand, among them de Lattre, who had been an outstanding divisional commander in the fighting and upon whom Weygand personally conferred the Grand Cross of the Legion of Honor at a special ceremony. De Lattre went on to command a military division district in the Vichy army.

A serious blow to those hoping for any ongoing resistance to Germany came with the Royal Navy's attack on the French Navy at Mers el-Kébir on July 3, 1940. One reason for the attack was to show that Great Britain intended to fight on with no holds barred, but in the subsequent outburst of furious Anglophobia the message was not heard. Pétain continued to believe that Germany would soon overwhelm Britain. Admiral Darlan, who claimed descent from a sailor in the French Navy at Trafalgar and had no liking for the British, launched an unsuccessful air attack on Gibraltar, and Laval pressed still harder for the change of alliances in favor of Germany.

In this atmosphere Weygand remained robust, even craftily using the Mers el-Kébir attack to try to strengthen his case for a military force in North Africa. He also secured permission from the Germans for a limited number of air passenger flights to North Africa, quarreled with Paul Baudouin, the colonial minister's policy of concession to the Japanese in Indochina, and strongly opposed the German decision to impose the costs of the Occupation on France. In a letter to Pétain dated July 16, Hitler, now realizing his earlier error, demanded eight air bases in Morocco, the use of ports in southern Unoccupied France, Algeria, Tunisia, and Morocco, the use of the Tunis–Casablanca railway line, and the establishment of metrological and radio stations in French Africa, all under the supervision of a German military commission. Huntziger sent Weygand a copy of the letter and the German president of the Armistice Commission added a further very arrogant note. A furious Weygand convinced the more resolute ministers in the Vichy government to send a courteously drafted but very firm rejection of the German demands, arguing that they were outside the terms of the armistice. Weygand's firmness on this issue was probably the decisive factor. If the Vichy government had given way, the consequences for Britain would have been daunting and quite possibly fatal.[4]

The second great French colonial territory under threat was Indochina. Here the Vichy government had attempted to resist Japanese claims by dismissing Catroux and replacing him with Admiral Jean Decoux, who fought increasingly pressing Japanese demands for access to airbases in Annam and the right to move troops through Tonkin. Decoux made a somewhat unrealistic request for military support to be sent to him, which even if the Germans would have permitted it was unlikely in view of their cordial relations with the Japanese. Weygand had to accept that the government had no option but to give way.

In French Central Africa, too, following the landing of the Gaullist Colonel Leclerc at Douala in Cameroon in late August, the five colonies of French Equatorial Africa began to fall to the Free French forces of de Gaulle, which were now steadily attracting a limited number of dedicated men and becoming an organization that posed a challenge to the legitimacy of the Pétain regime. Though the Royal Navy attempted to control access to the coast, little could be done to prevent the Gaullist expansion other than to make sure that the movement did not spread to the more important French West African colonies. In defense of the empire, Weygand issued orders that any British attempts to take over Syria or West Africa should be resisted, and in the case of West Africa that there should be reprisals against British colonies. At this time Weygand saw strict adherence to the armistice terms as the only way of constraining individual generals from violating them.

De Gaulle's Free France movement, slowly but steadily growing, became the subject of more serious discussion. Weygand and others believed that de Gaulle's disobedience could not be tolerated and was a threat to national unity. Weygand supported calls for a trial by a military court, and de Gaulle was demoted, given a prison sentence of four years, and assessed a large fine. After the arrival of news that Frenchmen supported by Britain had been ordered to fire on and kill other Frenchmen, de Gaulle's operations were seen as treason. He was stripped of French nationality and sentenced to death by a military tribunal; Weygand approved of the sentence.

In August a fresh misfortune had occurred in France itself. The German administration nominated two Germans as *gauleiters,* one for Alsace, the other for Lorraine. In the two regions the German language was immediately to replace French, and local young men were drafted into the German army, not the French. Not long after, the preliminary registration of Jews commenced. Weygand passionately protested the events in Alsace-Lorraine in council meetings, especially one on September 4 where he attacked Darlan and Laval, the latter replying abusively that Weygand's position as a minister was no longer tenable. The next day, Pétain, now convinced that collaboration was a necessity, informed Weygand that the Ministry of National Defense was to be abolished and a new ministry, combining National Defense and the army, was to be created. The prestige of Weygand was, however, still such that he could not be peremptorily dismissed, and such a dismissal might also connote that the French Army had been defeated with dishonor. Accordingly Pétain created a new almost vice-regal post for him, commander in chief and delegate general in North Africa. As well as moving him out of the way, the North African presence of Weygand was to be seen as a check on the possible spread of Gaullism from France's sub-Saharan African colonies. From the start, however, the Germans were not pleased with this appointment.

General Huntziger, whom Weygand trusted, was to replace him as minister and commander in chief and was in many of his actions to follow his predecessor's example. The aircraft carrying Weygand on a return journey from an inspection crash landed near Limoges. Weygand was quite seriously injured, a number of ribs being fractured. It was only after a month, on the 9th of October, that he was able to take up his new post.

During the time he was convalescing, the de Gaulle–inspired Anglo–Free French effort to seize Dakar and with it French West Africa had taken place on September 23 and 24 and had failed ignominiously. It had the effect of strengthening German beliefs that the Vichy forces could be relied upon to resist any further British attempts to gain a foothold in French North or West Africa, and also of increasing anti-British, pro-collaboration views in Vichy. It further added to the hatred of many, including

Weygand, of de Gaulle. Weygand himself added strength to his critics in Vichy by advising Pétain to ignore the pressure from Laval to meet with Hitler at Montoire and shake hands. Pétain did not follow Weygand's advice; it can be assumed that Laval told the Germans of Weygand's attitude if they were not already aware of it.

Controversy was to follow Weygand to Africa.

7

≕ ≕ ≕

A GENERAL OUT OF STEP: NORTH AFRICA
1940–41

Regarding much of Weygand's life, admirers pay their respects, sometimes perhaps too generously, detractors pour out their criticisms, often unjustly or harshly, and the small details of his daily life and work are not fully covered—for example, the impression Weygand made on individuals who were later to matter or on groups of soldiers whose impressions were apparently too insignificant to record. Above all, this is true in the period of Weygand's command in North Africa, where his presence, covert actions, and personal example were very real, but difficult to quantify and easy to belittle. He was to create an ethos: "We are not here just to defend North Africa, but to prepare to clear the enemy out of France." He always referred to the Germans as "les boches" and their activities as "les bocheries." His February 1941 secret instructions to regiments and garrisons concluded with exhortations to make every effort for their love of their country and their "longing for revenge," in particular to remember their duties, train hard, and keep fit. Improved morale and self-confidence had in fact already begun.

It was with a sense of relief to have escaped from the intrigues and cabals, and from collaborators and the ostentatious rich men who saw Vichy as a career opportunity, that Weygand arrived at Algiers on October 9, 1940, accompanied by Renée, who soon took over the work of the local Red Cross. For Weygand, command in North Africa quickly opened wider views of the world and the war than had been possible in the claustrophobic atmosphere of Vichy. Resentment over Mers el-Kébir and Dakar was still very strong, but the war situation was changing. The German air assault on Britain had not succeeded, and it seemed that plans for an invasion of England were being abandoned. The Italian Army's attempt to invade Egypt had failed totally; ten days after Weygand's arrival the Italian Navy was to suffer severely at the hands of the Royal Navy at Taranto. A glimpse of hope, albeit faint, could appear.

Weygand saw as his priority the retention of French colonial holdings in Africa intact and under legal French, in other words his, control. Italian or above all German intervention had to be prevented. But any overt public declaration of sympathy or support for Britain made in French North Africa or elsewhere would only lead to Axis intervention and therefore of necessity had to be forbidden or suppressed, a view that extended to negotiation with colonies that had become Gaullist. The governor-general of French West Africa at Dakar, Pierre Boisson, held the same views, and Weygand was able to strengthen his local authority. Both Weygand and Boisson were later to be much criticized for this hard but realistic assessment, some claiming it was largely personal. Others even went on to allege that de Gaulle rejoiced that Weygand had been driven into a corner; he had either to join with de Gaulle or forever be labeled a collaborator by Gaullists.[1] But for Weygand, de Gaulle remained the man who was sowing division at a time when unity had prospects of real gain; a further ingredient of which Weygand was probably aware was that in London de Gaulle was advising against giving Weygand much help, as it might discourage his Free French followers.

De Gaulle was in any case not among Weygand's major concerns, and attempts to define Weygand's work in the political context of his thirteen months in North Africa were constrained by three major factors. First, in Europe Hitler's priority strategy was now set—the Soviet Union and in particular Ukraine, which would commence with invasion on June 22, 1941. He might, and almost certainly did, have long-term projects for colonial expansion in Africa, and his naval staff wanted the use of Bizerte and Dakar, but for the moment Hitler wanted a secure, steady Western Europe for which a client Vichy French state kept in order by a small army was necessary. Italian and Spanish African ambitions would have to wait. German interests in North Africa were for the time being to be primarily economic. These priority interests became all the more pressing in the early autumn of 1941, when the German invasion of the Soviet Union first began to falter. The second context factor was that from February 1941 power in Vichy was in the hands of Admiral Darlan, vice president of the Council of Ministers and Pétain's "dauphin." Darlan's assessment of the war situation remained based on his firm belief that Germany would certainly win the war and be the dominant power in Europe for the foreseeable future. He remained, as he was throughout his entire life, a genuinely patriotic Frenchman, but his patriotism was biased and tragically misguided, and his dealings were often shady. He had no understanding at all of the military and naval power that the United States could develop and was convinced that the Soviet Union would collapse. With this strategic view he believed collaboration with the Germans, whom in fact he disliked even more than he disliked the British, was absolutely necessary and would secure concessions from Hitler for the present and an acceptable status for France in the postwar world. In his first months in power he increasingly saw Weygand as an obstruction to his policies and strategy, a general out of step. There was also a strong dimension of personal jealousy, Weygand having enjoyed a social and international-stage status before the war while Darlan was still making his career. He was continually to press his colleagues and Pétain for Weygand's removal, referring to Weygand as "le petit général."[2]

Weygand was fully aware of this and had either to temper or conceal much of his work on the ground and in reports to Vichy, and also to be very careful of whom he selected for his staffs. He nevertheless managed to send a secret congratulatory message to General Wavell after the British successes against the Italians in the winter of 1940–41.

Within the frame of these first two factors, the Germans were prepared to accept successive demands made by the Vichy minister for defense, Huntziger, and by Weygand for increases in troop levels in North Africa. To the Germans these French forces saved them the expenses of a garrison. At the same time the Germans realized that any attempt to use French forces in North Africa to reconquer the Equatorial African colonies taken over by de Gaulle would be disastrous. White settler political activity was allowed, although restricted to political parties permitted in Unoccupied France, while known Freemason groups or Spaniards taking refuge from the Franco regime were restrained and closely watched.

Weygand made evident his distrust of all, but in particular any figures of the extreme Right who favored collaboration. The treatment of the large, over 100,000-member, Jewish community in Algeria was, however, to be an unpleasant aspect of Weygand's tenure of office.[3] Algeria was considered to be a part of metropolitan France, not a protectorate like Morocco or Tunisia. In 1870 under the famous Crémieux Decree, the Jews in Algeria had been granted the right of French nationality. In keeping with the anti-Semitism of Vichy, the newly appointed minister of the interior, Marcel Peyrouton, in a first series of measures, abolished the 1870 decree, withdrawing the privilege of French nationality from Algerian Jews with only a very few exceptions, a measure drafted on October 6, three days before Weygand's arrival.

In a further measure on the 11th, Peyrouton prevented Jews from ever again applying for French nationality. Weygand had not been involved in any discussions about or preparation for this legislation, which in practice was designed to exclude all Jews including from positions as doctors and academics.

Knowing that Pétain had approved these measures, Weygand apparently did not feel that he could totally reject them, but in Weygand's time they were applied perfunctorily if at all. Several prefects, notably those in Oran and Constantine, the former appointed by the Blum Popular Front government, the latter a socialist, took little note, and elsewhere others turned blind eyes. Nevertheless, some Jews were packed off along with Republican Spanish refugees to labor camps. More were to follow later after the Germans had set up a special department for Jews in the Occupied Zone and wished to replicate such departments widely. In June 1941 measures stiffening those of October 1940 were directed for Algeria. These were meant to enforce a reduction, on average of 2 percent, in the presence of Jews in professions such as law and medicine; within the total numbers of Jews in schools an initial fourteen percent was soon lowered to seven percent. In August an extremist French official was sent out to seek to impose a general sequestration ("organization") of Jewish property, and Weygand was instructed to set up a local bureau for Algerian Jewish questions. While many *colons* welcomed the project, Weygand was unenthusiastic, and the confiscations and more brutal measures began only in December, after Weygand's recall.

The measures were very popular among the indigenous Muslim majority population, which may have eased Weygand's conscience in his need
for stability, and one of his views may well have been that the measures
prevented anti-Jewish riots. Certainly he was in no position to veto any
major Vichy measures of this kind, but he invested no personal interest or
drive in their pursuit, and Jewish lives, if not their welfare, were relatively
safe in the Weygand period. Only a very small number were sent back to
France on the trains to extermination camps. Nevertheless, his critics
would later argue that he should have taken much more positive action to
end the hardship and suffering.

In Morocco, which for long had a sizable, probably over 150,000, well-
respected mainly Sephardic Jewish community, the French Resident-
General, General Noguès, supported by Weygand and also the young
Sultan, Sidi Mohammed V, together with enlightened protectorate officials, all contrived to see that the German anti-Jewish measures were either ignored or at least carried out very perfunctorily. Jewish schools kept
their pupils and teachers; there was no "organization" of Jewish properties
and no forcing of Jews into urban ghettos. In Tunisia, where Weygand and
the French Resident, Admiral Jean-Pierre Esteva, had only to deal with
Italian armistice officials, who were totally uninterested in and sometimes
opposed to anti-Jewish policies, the smaller Jewish communities only very
rarely faced harassment.

The indigenous people, although becoming increasingly nationalistic,
generally saw French rule for the time being as necessary, preferable to
the Italians or the Spaniards. In particular the French were respected in
Morocco, where the French administration in the tradition of the first
Resident-General, Hubert Lyautey, had preserved local Moslem institutions and culture, and the Berber chieftains helped with the concealment
of weapons. Sultan Sidi Mohammed was well abreast of affairs and had no
illusions about foreign control; the appalling brutality of the concentrated
mustard gas attacks by the Spanish Army in Spanish Morocco in the 1920s
and 1930s was well-known to him. Later after Weygand's recall and the
American entry into the war, nationalism increased, locally in North Africa expressing itself as an opportunity to display preference for de Gaulle.

The third important context framing Weygand's months in North
Africa was economic; the territories, in particular Algeria with its large

settler populations, were heavily dependent on external trade for their consumer goods—petrol, lamp and gas oil, coal, cotton goods, condensed milk, cheap tea, and sugar. But the French territories were faced with a British blockade of Moroccan ports and the Strait of Gibraltar. American help was sought, but the Americans made it clear that as a basis for any agreement they did not wish to see a German military presence in North or West Africa. The British government was opposed to any help being given. From the start Weygand was very much aware of the local problems and shortages and was greatly encouraged when at American insistence and following a friendly letter from Churchill to Weygand, the British lifted their naval blockade. The lifting was on the condition that British merchant ships being held in Moroccan ports were released and that there would be no reexport of strategic materials from North Africa to the *métropole*.

On February 26, 1941, Weygand concluded an agreement with Robert J. Murphy, a diplomat who had been formerly at the American embassy in Paris but who had been sent to watch developments in North Africa.[4] Murphy formed a very high regard for Weygand, and the two men trusted each other fully. Under the agreement twelve special American officials designated as "vice-consuls" were posted to ensure that cargoes, in particular rubber, were not moved on elsewhere. Weygand freely told Murphy that he hoped for an Allied victory and arranged for the reports of the American officials to Washington to have diplomatic security privilege status, with no doubt some intelligence material added for their eyes. The consuls were at first assisted by little groups of French officers and officials in Algeria opposed to the armistice. The indigenous populations were impressed by Weygand's interest in small-holding level agricultural development, country roads, wells, local markets, and irrigation dams, and his encouragement for the expansion of groundnut and oil-seed growing. The 1940–41 harvest, too, was unusually bountiful.

On his arrival Weygand found the military disorganized and demoralized. Local forces had been weakened by drafts sent to France in May. Many soldiers returning from France were wounded or unfit, and many were disillusioned. A few had been turned by German propaganda. Demobilization was chaotic. Hurriedly put together units lacked any esprit de corps. Weygand felt that he was visiting depots rather than regiments, and at first surreptitious reorganization was forbidden. On paper the military strength at the armistice was one of five underequipped and below-strength divisions plus Mareth Line fortress troops, also below strength, on the Tunis/Libya border. Other garrison units were in little better condition. Some units on the Spanish/Moroccan border were still equipped with pre-1914 rifles. Of the three tank regiments, two still had the 1917 Renault light tanks. There were also a few internal security units, including some riding camel companies and in Morocco a number of semiregular goums.[5] The best regiments were the one cavalry and three infantry regiments of the Foreign Legion, from which the Germans soon demanded the repatriation of German members, which the French refused. Under German pressure, they conceded the release only of the few who volunteered.

The morale of the 17e Algerian Tirailleurs, reduced to dirty uniforms and poor food with their prewar pride in and respect for their regiments lost, had, however, been badly shaken, the men no longer enjoying their former prestige and also social status among relatives and communities. On January 25, 1941 eight hundred Algerian Tirailleurs mutinied near Algiers, took weapons from their armory, murdered a number of French officers and NCOs, and then took to the streets. There, proclaiming jihad, they killed 23 civilians, including women, and wounded over a 130 more. The regiment had been badly officered, and an Algerian intelligence officer led the mutiny. Some of the Tirailleurs had been German prisoners and subjected to propaganda.[6] Shooting in the streets followed and lasted for several days before French forces restored order. Nine leading mutineers were executed in a public square by firing squads drawn from different regiments. The shooting was not immediately effective in all cases. In the following three months of courts-martial a further twenty-three mutineers were executed and more sentenced to forced labor.

Axis armistice administration in Africa was initially left to the Italians, with a commission headquarters in Tunis. The majority of the officers were inefficient and behaved with an arrogance that at times bordered on the ridiculous. The total number of troops permitted for North Africa was at first limited to 30,000, simply for internal security duties and limited to Algeria only. The French used the events of Mers el-Kébir and Dakar to request an expansion to 100,000 plus 20,000 unarmed laborers for North Africa and 33,000 for West Africa. A little later the West Africa total was nominally raised to 56,000, in practice discreetly to over 90,000. In North Africa the total was increased to 120,000 but including the goums, which were no longer to be counted as "police." By April 1941 Weygand had secured a further increase to 127,000 together with 16,000 goums.[7] After the British invasion of Syria, a regiment of Moroccan Tirailleurs, together with other support units destined to support the French Syrian garrison, enabled a further 6,400 troops to be added. The Vichy youth organization, the Chantiers de la Jeunesse, was given more and more military training in addition to its eight-month labor duties. The organization, compulsory for all nineteen-year-old fit men, became very popular; boys falsified their age to join as volunteers. Later, in 1942, whole units were to complete military training. By the time of Weygand's departure the total number of soldiers trained or under training in the three North African territories was over 170,000.

In January 1941 Weygand addressed a formal request to Pétain asking for the dispatch from France of a number of machine guns, mortars, light armored vehicles, and spare parts, and the release from German prisons of a number of officers. He also expressed his wish to expand the number of West African Tirailleurs. The letter was passed to Huntziger, who took no action. In further letters later Weygand deployed an argument that strengthening his local forces was necessary to protect the territories, especially the coastlines, from a British invasion, clearly a pretext that he thought more likely to appeal to Vichy. Again he met with no success.

In June, following special pressure on Vichy mounted by Weygand, the Germans released, to his surprise, the outstandingly able and experienced General Alphonse Juin from prison, together with a number of other officers and NCOs with African experience. Weygand was then able to have three excellent officers who shared his views in place for several key months; Juin in Algiers, de Lattre in Tunis, and Koeltz in Morocco.

The French enjoyed frustrating the attempts at inspection made by officers of the Italian Armistice Commission. They demanded that inspecting officers give forty-eight hours' notice of their plans, with precise details of their travel routes. The officers were permitted to put questions only to French officers and not to soldiers. Generous—and protracted—hospitality was to be given them, along with access to facilities for riding, hunting, sightseeing, and relaxation. In return handsome Italian officers tried to exercise their charms on the daughters of settlers who might have access to the French military. When the Germans joined the work of the commission in January 1941 their officers were found to be less thorough and more relaxed, often in need of relaxation after a tour in the Soviet Union, but were nevertheless watched more closely. On meeting one German general, Weygand was so chilly and haughty that one observer felt the German must have wondered who had won the 1940 campaign.

A considerable quantity of weaponry and ammunition was concealed during the Weygand years. The numbers claimed vary. French loyalists after the war cited high figures to boost their own status; the German figures were lower because they were probably incomplete.[8] The totals claimed by Weygand follow with the German totals next in parentheses:

Rifles 55,000 (45,000)
Submachine carbines 1,500 (1,350)
Machine guns 2,500 (1,380)
Mortars 310 (165)
75mm field guns 82 (41)
Other small cannons (35)
47mm antitank guns 43 (31)
Tanks 12 (5)

An attempt to produce armored cars locally resulted in a few very unsatisfactory machines. The quality and totals were far short of those needed for effective divisions, but were of use in training.

Weygand was much concerned with the danger that a severe defeat for the Afrika Korps and the Italians might lead them to retreat into Tunisia and there assert full political and military control. Much of the Mareth Line defense had been taken down on instructions from the Armistice Commission, and Weygand's border units were neither strong enough nor equipped to stop German armored units on the frontier. Weygand therefore had a plan prepared for a holding defense line further inland, based on the eastern end of the Atlas mountain range, through Tebessa to the sea west of Bizerte, a line to be held until reinforcements arrived from Algeria and Morocco.

He was fortunate to have the services of a highly skilled intelligence officer, Commandant Henri Navarre (later to be the French commander in Indochina at the time of Dien Bien Phu in 1954), assisted by the very able Commandant Jean Chrétien as his principal intelligence aides. One of Navarre's main concerns was the passing of shipping-movement intelligence to the British. In use of naval intelligence facilities, however, information collected had to be described as needed for "statistical purposes" as Weygand was concerned that the naval operators might withhold the data if they knew it was going to be passed to the British. Among their early intelligence successes was a report that led to the sinking of an Italian oil tanker and reports that led to the sinking of supply ships for the arriving Afrika Korps. Later a system was set up to observe the movements of Italian supply ships that were seeking safety by sailing close to the Tunisian coast and taking refuge at Sfax. Reports were sent on to the Royal Navy light cruiser HMS *Aurora* based at Malta.[9] However, with Mers el-Kébir still very much in mind, the marine officers were not always supportive of Weygand, and instead looked to Darlan for leadership. Friction resulted, in particular between Weygand and the governor-general of Algeria, Admiral Abrial.

The army's intelligence service, SR, also maintained a close counter-intelligence security watch, using post and telecommunications staff as well as military personnel. German agents identified were arrested and sentenced, some, particularly if Arab, to death, Weygand having first telephoned Pétain to persuade him not to grant clemency.

Weygand also had to face problems from his compatriots. In November 1940 the very senior General Catroux, who had joined de Gaulle, tried to make contact with Weygand. To avoid the watchful eyes of the Axis agents, Weygand sent Navarre to Tangiers to meet Catroux's emissary. Nothing came from the meeting, which remained polite, Catroux paying full respect to Weygand.

In January 1941 Churchill sent a friendly letter concerning petrol, which included a hope for cooperation; Weygand did not reply. At the end of February, de Gaulle himself wrote a courteous and respectful letter to Weygand. Transmitted via the British consul in Tangiers, the letter urged a united common front. Weygand did not reply. Quite apart from his dislike of de Gaulle as an upstart rebel whose actions simply worsened an already difficult situation, Weygand correctly assessed that were he able to join de Gaulle, Britain would not have the military strength to prevent a German reprisal occupation of French North Africa. Correct though Weygand may have been, his spurning of de Gaulle and his preference to deal with "Anglo-Saxon" Americans served to widen irretrievably de Gaulle's opposition to him.

Equally unreal was a conspiracy in March 1941 that included a civilian businessman, Jacques Lemaigre-Dubreuil, Colonel Georges Loustaunau-Lacau, and Commandant André Beaufre, and a handful of other military officers and civilian officials.[10] The conspiracy aimed to set up an arrangement, more than somewhat vague, for importing American weaponry. The plot was detected, and Loustaunau-Lacau whose views were apt to change, "returned to France." Weygand wished to impose minor disciplinary measures upon Beaufre, but the authorities in Vichy demanded arrest and imprisonment. For this Beaufre never reproached Weygand, and on his release he always expressed his admiration for him; one suspects that the prison conditions may not have been severe.

In the spring a much more serious sequence of events followed. An Arab nationalist, Rashid al Gailani, planned to lead an uprising against the British in Iraq. The Germans, anxious to help, held talks with Darlan in early May, the admiral meeting Hitler personally at Berchtesgaden on the 11th and 12th of May. He followed this with a violently anti-British broadcast, concluding with an allegorical observation that if British troops entered Paris all they would find there would be a cemetery. After two weeks of negotiation agreement was reached, to the satisfaction of Darlan but greeted with apprehension by Huntziger. The agreement, known as the Protocols of Paris, signed on May 28 provided for French cooperation with the Germans in Syria to assist al Gailani, the use of the port of Bizerte in Tunisia, the sale of some vehicles and artillery to the Germans for their use by the Afrika Korps, and the use of the port of Dakar after necessary defensive preparations for German merchant shipping. The use of facilities was extended later to include those needed for submarines for the German Navy. In return for these concessions the Germans were to grant some easing of conditions in the Occupied Zone and liberation for French Army prisoners of war, some 72,000 still being held captive in Germany. The deal was specifically planned to be the basis of a new relationship in which France would become an associate of Germany in the war. Darlan remained convinced the Axis powers would be the winners.

Predictably, Weygand was furious. He hurried off to Vichy armed with an irate ten-page letter to Pétain roundly condemning French cooperation with those whom he referred to as "adversaries" and arguing forcefully that implementation of the Protocols would lead to open conflict in North Africa. Among members of the Vichy cabinet he was supported by Boisson and Esteva, and after three days he emerged to claim that he had halted the agreement. Apparently at one point he had asserted that if the Germans attempted to take over bases in Africa, whatever his government might say, he would order armed resistance.[11]

This may well have been the case at Vichy, but more realistic was the Germans' own preoccupation with their plans for the attack on the Soviet Union and the likely inability of their forces to spare manpower and resources to hold Dakar against Gaullist reaction to their arrival. Better to have Weygand in charge than an actively hostile de Gaulle. The Germans were, however, able to draw consolation from the wave of anti-British feeling that followed the British invasion of Syria that opened on June 8, 1941. The local French garrison's resistance, although eventually overcome, had been led by General Henri Dentz; collaborationists soon began to speak of him as a suitable replacement for Weygand in Africa. The American intervention to take military authority in Iceland led the Germans to wonder whether they might not decide to intervene also at Dakar. Despite the resentments over Syria, obstructions were placed in the path of German hopes for the use of Bizerte—French warships could not provide cover so that German supplies would have to be loaded in Italian ports, not Toulon or Marseilles. The failure of the Protocols project was not entirely the work of Weygand, but his part in reducing the proposed new partnership to waste paper was an important one.

In German eyes, however, Weygand was an enemy. Hitler had earlier remarked that no Habsburg prince could ever be a friend of Germany, and German pressure on Vichy for his replacement mounted. To this Darlan was more than willing to add his name. Until September Pétain shielded Weygand, but in October under intense German pressure and a threat of resignation from Darlan if Weygand was not removed, he gave way. At first he offered Weygand a consolation post, clearly designed to be one with no power, as a minister for the empire, or he could accept limitation of his powers in North Africa to civil matters. But after learning that in an unguarded moment Weygand had expressed the hope that the Russian campaign would destroy Germany, Pétain decided that he could no longer cover for him. On November 18 in Vichy, Weygand was told of his dismissal. He would not be employed again and must live in France, and he could not return to North Africa for any farewells. The Germans, however, were not able to secure the bitterly anti-British Dentz as his replacement. Instead the redoubtable General Juin was promoted, not as a vice-regal delegate for both North and West Africa, but only as commander in chief of ground, air, and coastal defense forces in the three North African territories. Darlan believed that overall authority was best divided, and he retained all control of the navy for himself. Juin had first been offered the post of minister for war in place of Huntziger, who had just been killed in an aircraft accident, but he had replied that he wanted to serve only in Africa. Juin was shocked by Weygand's dismissal and upon his appointment made clear the strategy of his command with his historic words "Messieurs, la séance continue." Early in February he followed up this declaration with a secret and personal instruction to his senior commanders, clearly setting out that the Axis armies were France's enemy and that they might invade Tunisia either from Libya or from an assault launched from Sicily.[12]

"La séance continue" was an indirect tribute to Weygand's thirteen months as a "general out of step." He had been accused of defeatism in May 1940; the accusation was not to be heard in his time in North Africa. There, from the start of his command, he had seen the three territories and a French military power growing within them as a vital check on further German strategy for the war, and above all the foundation for the restoration of the French Army for an eventual overthrow of Germany and that liberation of France. He left Africa sad and bitter, but his achievement was later to be called "L'Armeé de Weygand."[13]

8

⇥ ⇥ ⇥

FINAL MISFORTUNES AND FINAL YEARS
1941–65

Following his dismissal Weygand was soon joined by Renée and his son
Jacques, both also banned from staying in North Africa. His long-time
military secretary, Commandant Gasser, and his aide-de-camp, Lieutenant de Leusse, were allowed to return to Algiers. His biographer records
that on bidding them farewell Weygand remarked, obviously with de
Gaulle's forces' activities in Syria and Africa in mind, "Listen my loyal
helpers, I will never order Frenchmen to open fire on other Frenchmen,
I will never take such a responsibility. I do not have the right. I am not
French, I am not French." Whether this comment was made in not unreasonable emotion, made deliberately for the record, or possibly both
will never be known.[1]

The first roof over the Weygand family's head was the villa owned by
the Count and Countess de Leusse family, known critics of any form
of collaboration. The family soon moved to the Parc-Hotel at Grasse,
where his aides quickly noticed they were continually watched by Vichy police agents. There, after Pearl Harbor, Weygand was visited by a
diplomat from the American embassy at Vichy, Douglas MacArthur, the
nephew of the Pacific War general, bringing both a letter dated December
27, 1941, and a personal message from President Roosevelt.[2] The letter
spoke of Roosevelt's continuing respect for Weygand and regret that he
had been recalled from Africa and of the successes (soon to be undone)
of the British Army in Libya and of the Red Army on the Eastern Front.
Roosevelt continued with an assurance that the United States, now at war

but not against France, would devote its work to the repatriation of France and French power.

MacArthur then set out in greater detail American policy, starting firmly that the United States would mount a preventive operation if there was a threat of German occupation of French North Africa and also very probably if bases were conceded to the Germans, if Pétain was replaced by an out-and-out collaborationist, or if French warships were used against the U.S. Navy. The nub of the mission then emerged: in the event of any of those situations arising, would Weygand be willing to return to command in North Africa, to lead and coordinate a rally of the population and the local military in an alliance with the United States and other allies, and move forward to the defeat of the Germans and the liberation of France? American records note that Weygand declined the offer firmly but politely. Weygand's own memoirs, while noting the visit, do not mention the offer of a return to command. Ending the discussion, MacArthur requested that it all be kept secret, to which Weygand replied that he would have to tell Pétain but could give an assurance that it would go no further. For Weygand, Pétain was still the high authority, and Roosevelt's offer, if he accepted, would have meant disloyalty and disobedience. One may surmise that his age, now seventy-five, and the events of the last two years had also played a part in his decision and that he felt that active service was now beyond him. He and his family moved to a house he had rented in Cannes, where many people, civil and military, visited him, but where police surveillance became more disturbing.

Weygand remained for another few months active as an adviser, with access to Pétain and contacts elsewhere in the Vichy establishment. In his memoirs he describes an early March 1942 meeting with Pétain, who appeared in good health, fully aware of the course of events, and determined to remain in power.[3] A curious and still far from clear event took place in the summer of 1942 when, apparently unknown to both Churchill and de Gaulle, a senior Vichy Army colonel made a secret visit to the British War Office and MI6, the Secret Intelligence Service, in London. The colonel's mission was to try to secure equipment for the Vichy Army so that it could act in support of a British or Allied invasion of France. For such an operation, secret plans for the mobilization of the Vichy Army were in hand. Weygand was one of the supporters of this project. Whether it was instigated by the chief of staff of the Vichy Army is not clear; it might have been a faction that could be disowned if the mission had been discovered. It was in any case overtaken by the Allied side's planning for the North African landings later in the year.

In June 1942 Weygand received a direct invitation to join up with de Gaulle delivered by René Massigli, a diplomat who had his own contacts. Weygand again refused. His loyalty to Pétain, though, was coming under great strain as he had found the Marshal ever more secretive. On June 22 Laval, who had replaced Darlan as vice president in April, made an open statement clearly hoping for a German victory. On hearing that Pétain had given his approval for this statement, Weygand in a white-hot rage tore up the signed photograph of the Marshal given to him by the increasingly frail old man.

The Allied landings in Morocco and Algeria on November 8, 1942, caused total confusion at Vichy, particularly as Darlan, still as the titular commander in chief of all French forces, was in Africa on a visit.[4] It appears that Darlan had now come to realize that the Axis was after all not going to win the war; a date for this conversion may well have been the American naval victory at Midway in June. His visit to Algeria was ostensibly to see his son in hospital but it had wider purposes, although Darlan did not know of the proximity of the Anglo-American action. Once the invasion commenced, Algiers became the stage for passionate debate over who was in command, whether resistance to the invasion should be continued, or whether a ceasefire should be negotiated, all in the absence of clear instructions from Pétain at Vichy and under vigorous pressure from the Americans.

At 9.00 AM on the morning of November 8 Weygand received a telephone call from his son Jacques, recently appointed a liaison colonel for the Vichy government, who told his father that Pétain wished to see him. Wondering whether this might portend some new command and, if so, whether should he accept, he accordingly set off from Cannes to the airfield at Saint-Raphael, where he was told an aircraft awaited him. When Weygand arrived at the airfield he found the entrance gates closed, and a navy captain told him that he would not be permitted to fly to North Africa. Weygand protested that he had no intention of flying to North Africa, that the Marshal had ordered him to Vichy. The captain replied that the pilot had arrived with no clear orders. Eventually Weygand was allowed to take off—but with a naval lieutenant armed with a revolver sitting beside him to ensure the flight headed north. Prior to his departure Weygand said farewell to Renée, little knowing how long it would be before he would see her again.

In Vichy the collaborationists, headed by Laval and backed by General Brideaux, the war minister, and Admiral Platon, were concerned that no French action appearing to sympathize with the Allied invasion should be allowed to harm relations with the Germans. More resolute voices saw this as the opening of an opportunity for France. Laval threatened resignation if France agreed to any armistice with the Americans. Weygand urged Pétain at least to order an end to the local French naval and military opposition to the Americans, to order the Armistice Army out of barracks and into remote mountains or rural areas, and to order the fleet in Toulon to sail for Algerian ports. Although he did not tell Weygand, Pétain, under pressure from the Germans, sent an open message ordering continuing resistance to the Allies. However, it has been claimed, probably correctly but without absolute certainty, that in a secret coded message Pétain approved the local ceasefire that Admiral Platon had authorized. Orders for the Armistice Army to leave barracks led to reconnaissance but nothing further, and no order was given to the fleet to put to sea, as it was feared that this act would lead immediately to open conflict with Germany. Even Weygand's milder proposal that the fleet should sail to Spanish waters was thought too dangerous. During the day the first German troops were flown into Tunisia.

The situation took a considerable turn for the worse when on November 11 the Germans decided to occupy Unoccupied France. Only a small detachment of the Vichy Army under de Lattre attempted even a token resistance—for which de Lattre was later court-martialed. Sent to prison, de Lattre escaped with the aid of his teenage son and was flown to England. Weygand apparently made a final effort to persuade the Marshal to consider flying to North Africa, offering to accompany him, and there openly declare for the Allied cause or at least make a broadcast for the world to hear to protest Germany's breach of the terms of the armistice. Pétain agreed to make a stiff protest to Field Marshal Gerd von Rundstedt, due to visit Vichy, and a national broadcast. He delivered the protest, in part drafted by Weygand, but the broadcast was not made. Whether he changed his mind or his mind was changed for him is not clear. On advice from General Joseph de La Porte du Theil of the Chantiers de la Jeunesse, Pétain decided that he must remain in France to stand by and suffer with the nation and that it would be cowardice to leave. There was honor in the decision, and it was almost certainly reached honorably within the thinking of a very old man afraid of aircraft journeys. It was, however, to cost him the last chance of retrieving the reputation of the man to whom in earlier years France had owed so much. Historians were to have the Jewish persecution and the paramilitary Milice in the forefront of their minds when reviewing Pétain's Vichy years, an attitude reflecting once again the radical side of the national fault line.

On the morning of November 12, Pétain told Weygand that he had no further duties for him. He advised Weygand not to return to Cannes as there were large numbers of German troops along the coast, but to stay in the town of Guéret for a few days and plan to move his family home there. At a final meeting with Pétain, at which Laval and the Police Ministry secretary general were present, the latter told Weygand how anxious the German authorities were to arrest him.[5] He strongly argued to Laval that France was now clearly on the wrong side in the war. There followed a fare-well lunch, and after some delay, accompanied by his son and daughter-in-law, Catherine, they set off for Guéret. Pétain provided an official car, and a second car containing three police officers followed behind. Fifteen minutes later a large German car containing a German ss officer and two soldiers flashed past them, turned round, and blocked the road. The officer got out of the car, accompanied by a soldier with a submachine gun, and a second car containing three more plainclothes German policemen, all armed with submachine guns, drew up. The ss captain announced that in the name of the Führer he was arresting Weygand. With Weygand directed to the ss captain's car and his son and daughter-in-law following in the Marshal's vehicle, they were all driven to Moulins. There, they were given dinner apart, after which Weygand was told to say good-bye to his family. He was then driven off to Radolfzell, on the shores of Lake Constance, to be held under the German code name for him, Lotterman, in an ss training barracks. Pétain protested strongly to the German foreign secretary, Joachim von Ribbentrop, and was told that the conditions of his detention should be considered extraordinarily humane.[6] Certainly, until his move to Austria in late 1943, he was generally treated well; no doubt the Germans did not wish to face French public opinion were Weygand to die in captivity. He was, however, pestered by jibes from the young ss officers and questioned about Laval, whom his questioners hoped he would deride; Weygand replied simply that Laval was a Frenchman and he had nothing to say about him. Depressed and fearing that his life was drawing to a close, in December he wrote a memorandum summing up his life as a failure and saying that he was leaving no achievement behind him, an indication of the strain captivity was putting on him. Yet at the same time he began preparing notes for a future memoir, which he was able to keep from both German and French attention. Back at Vichy Renée, Jacques, and Catherine all petitioned for his release, in vain.

In January 1943 the Germans moved him to a country house at Garlitz, forty-five miles from Hamburg. There Renée was allowed to join him, and she remained with him until May 1945. At Garlitz he was guarded by an ss captain, twenty soldiers, and two dogs. Conditions were spartan, as were conditions generally in Germany, but they were far worse in many prisoner-of-war camps. The local Mecklenburg area of Germany was Lutheran and Weygand found attendance at Mass impossible, but at Easter 1943 a Roman Catholic priest was sent from Berlin to hear confessions and celebrate Mass. Day by day, the ss guards kept up a steady stream of jibes and coarse jokes. On the 12th of each month—the 12th being the day of the month of his arrest—Weygand wrote a letter of protest, which was ignored, and he further annoyed the Germans by refusing to write a letter denouncing "bolshevism."

At the end of 1943, the Germans moved Weygand to an Austrian castle at Itter, near Kitzbühel. His company there included, among others, Reynaud, Daladier, Gamelin, de la Rocque, and Michael Clemenceau, the son of the former prime minister. Weygand and Renée were not well received, as old controversies were remembered. Weygand's biographer describes the little group as a "basket of crabs." Separate meal tables had to be arranged; Renée was treated with haughty disdain. With the passing of time and more knowledge of the others' actions tension eased a little, but Weygand and Renée's table was joined only by de la Rocque, Jean Borotra, a French national tennis champion and Wimbledon singles winner in 1924 and 1926 who had been a Vichy minister until his dismissal in 1941, and the former trade union leader Léon Jouhaux and his wife.

At the end of April 1945, as the American forces approached Tyrol, Borotra escaped, only to be quickly recaptured. On May 5 he escaped again, disguised as a farm laborer, and made contact with elements of General Anthony McAuliffe's 103rd Division. In the final clash that followed, the roof of the castle was damaged, and the detainees eventually released. They identified themselves before McAuliffe and were given a very good welcome dinner. On the 7th, they were taken to the headquarters of General de Lattre de Tassigny's victorious First Army at Lindau on the shores of Lake Constance, where de Lattre was giving a dinner party for his senior officers.[7]

De Lattre was faced with an acutely embarrassing situation; he owed much to Weygand and greatly respected him. But he had earlier received telegram instructions from de Gaulle to place anyone who had served in a Vichy administration under arrest, adding that whatever his own feelings might be, de Lattre was to send Weygand to Paris under escort. The party arrived from Itter just as the dinner commenced, and they were welcomed by a band and a guard of honor, respect due to Reynaud and Daldier as former prime ministers. Sadly, Weygand thought that it was in his honor. Reynaud was taken away by de Lattre; Weygand and Renée were left to wait with no one attending to their luggage. After a while de Lattre reappeared and took Weygand and Renée to rooms, talked with them for a few minutes, but made no mention of de Gaulle's orders.

Early on the next morning de Lattre was woken with instructions to proceed to Berlin at once to represent France at the final surrender of the Germans. The original plan for this ceremony had been limited to the United States, the Soviet Union, and Great Britain, but British Air Marshal Lord Tedder had argued at the last minute for the inclusion of France.[8] At 2:00 AM de Lattre woke Weygand to tell him this news, and also of de Gaulle's orders. He then departed, having promised Weygand a farewell guard of honor and band, and the use of his car to take him and Renée to Paris.

On his arrival in Paris Weygand was taken into custody, charged with attempts against the internal security of the state and of anti-Republican attitudes, and transported to a police remand center on the Quai des

Orfèvres. There he was lodged, with Borotra as a roommate, in a room furnished with camp beds, a wash basin, and a bucket of water, together with the prospect of being moved to the Fresnes prison for hardened criminals. However, his elder son, Edouard, mobilized the support of leading lawyers and secured his removal to the famous Val-de-Grâce military hospital with its magnificent seventeenth-century chapel. There, even if under guard, Weygand was treated with some dignity and kept in safety until May 6, 1946, when he was released.

In these months, with more to follow, the bitterness of French politics was once again to be shown to the French public and the wide world, particularly after the conviction of Pétain for treason. The civil-military rift of 1940 was also reappearing. The Communist Party was enjoying the credit that it earned from its participation in the Resistance (from June 22, 1941) and the socialists were also strong. France's position in the war was being presented as de Gaulle and the Resistance on the side of the good, Pétain and Vichy on the side of the bad. Pétain and Weygand were obvious targets. Weygand was called to give evidence at the trial of Pétain, which opened in June, 1945. Released from the Val-de-Grâce to attend and leaning on a walking stick, he mounted a robust defense of Pétain's policies with which he was associated by his call for an armistice in June 1940, his service in Pétain's first government as a minister, and his refusal to lead North and West Africa into the de Gaulle camp.[9] His exchanges with Reynaud were especially vitriolic.

Weygand himself was summoned to appear before a High Court of Justice, a creation of de Gaulle, in November 1945, the first meeting taking place in the Val-de-Grâce.[10] In his case the court was initially composed of twelve members of the 1940 legislature that had approved the passing of supreme powers to Pétain, and twelve members of the Resistance. (The membership of the court was to change over its long period of existence.) Skilled lawyers, however, rallied to Weygand's decision to contest the charges against him. A charge that he had not obeyed a policy directive issued by de Gaulle on June 12, 1940, requiring measures to be prepared to continue the war in North Africa was rebutted with the argument that it was not a categorical order. A challenge denying Weygand's assertion that he had recommended the fleet to put to sea was dismissed on the grounds that after six years the evidence was obscure. An accusation that Weygand had banned any relationship with any person who worked with a foreign government, that is, de Gaulle, was dropped when it was discovered that the relevant order had in fact been issued by Pétain and not Weygand. The whole issue of the armistice, over which Weygand had been apprehensive and in connection with which Weygand was being charged with having contact with the enemy, was brushed aside after violent ill-tempered exchanges with Reynaud. The verdict was that Weygand had not been solely responsible for the armistice and if the charge was pursued further President Lebrun and his ministers would have to be involved. Accusations that in the 1930s Weygand and also Pétain conspired against the Republic were dismissed as improbable in view of the age of both. Foch's widow, de Lattre, and officers of Weygand's North Africa staff all appeared as defense witnesses for Weygand. Summing up, the *procureur général* stated that Weygand had acted honorably and not directly involved himself in politics, and that though Weygand had been guilty of membership in Pétain's government as minister for war, he had atoned for this by his work in North Africa, in particular his opposition to the 1941 Protocols. In June 1946 he was allowed to go to his Paris apartment, to the fury of the communist and socialist members of the court, which continued with periodic meetings that achieved nothing, until Weygand was given a final acquittal on May 6, 1948. During all this time he was kept under police supervision.

The acquittal was timely. His pay as a general, which had been authorized for life in 1932, had been stopped June 1, 1945, by order of de Gaulle, followed a few days later by a legal sequestration of his property and the freezing of his bank accounts. Since that time, Weygand and his family had been entirely dependent on friends for support.

His legal troubles were unfortunately not limited to the High Court of Justice; he was directed to appear before a Parliamentary Enquiry Commission concerning events between 1939 and 1945. The commission's membership was mixed; some members were from parliament, others were Resistance figures, but all were institutionally prejudiced against Weygand. His first appearance before the commission was on July 25, 1947, and he received ten more summons to appear between March and June 1949.

Weygand was now over eighty. Many of the sessions were protracted, sometimes running late in the evening and into the night. His principal attacker, Charles Serre, was a Dachau concentration camp survivor. He was supported by Lucien Aubrac, a Resistance hero, and a political philosopher, Louis Marin. Weygand was attacked on all of his activities from 1930 onward: why he had not pressed for more men and equipment in the early 1930s, to which Weygand answered with memoranda and documents, and then again in the later 1930s, to which Weygand replied that he was not in power and no one asked him for advice, not even on the twentieth anniversary of the 1918 armistice. He was challenged on the optimism he expressed in late 1939, to which he answered that it was not his business to undermine Gamelin. He went on to note the costs and delays of French industry in tank manufacture, delays sometimes worsened by changes in staff requirements. He was taken to task on the Ardennes breakthrough, which he answered by reminding the commission of France's lack of aircraft, and over the armistice in which charges were biased against him. He had little difficulty in rejecting de Gaulle's charge that he failed to evacuate 500,000 men to North Africa by pointing out that neither the men nor the ships were available.

With respect to his attitude toward de Gaulle and the Free French generals, Weygand took the line of argument that his concern was to prevent disorder and confusion in the French Empire, but he was criticized over the Beaufre affair. Overall his defense was patchy, age and strain telling heavily upon him, but a number of generals of the Liberation Army, including de Lattre and Joseph de Goislard de Monsabert, came out to support him. He was reproved for his interesting and very personal suggestion that the motto for the post-armistice French state should be amended to read "Dieu, la Patrie, la Famille, le Travail" instead of "Travail, Famille, Patrie," not so much for the changes but as indicating his identifying with the Vichy regime. Weygand replied that he was a soldier who had never meddled in politics. It was not an argument that satisfied the anticlericals, and even less did his defense of Pétain as a solid defender of the Republic. The argument became more theoretical and abstract, including what the role of the state should be, and there were allegations of malign intentions behind some of Weygand's decisions. At his last appearance, Weygand said rather testily that if the commission stated in its report that this old sweat (*brute*) came to us to say he was no philosopher they could go ahead, he would not care, he was an old man who had acted in the way that he thought he should and had nothing further to add. In a written note he added that he had never experienced a government with an army that matched its policies, nor an army that the government and nation actually needed, that discussion of intentions was irrelevant, and that for the defeat of 1940 ultimately the climate of opinion of the whole French nation must carry the blame.[11]

Interest in France in these arguments was, however, now beginning to wane. New and bitter controversies were opening around the counterinsurgency campaign in Madagascar and the expanding war in Indochina, and more generous and tolerant views were now being taken concerning the events of the war.

In the summer of 1951 a member of the legislature drafted a proposal that Generals Weygand, de Lattre, and Juin should be awarded the title of Marshal of France. Juin, in thanking the deputy, strongly supported the inclusion of Weygand. Weygand himself, however, asked that his name be withdrawn, saying that though he had helped to build an army he had himself not led it into battle.[12]

Weygand still retained a close interest in national affairs, particularly any relating to the army. He disliked the Fourth Republic and the endless changes of government reminiscent of the 1920s and 1930s and was actually heard on one occasion to express a hope that de Gaulle might return to power. He opposed the concept of the European Defense Community with a European, non-national army, as did Juin, now the only living Marshal of France, and de Gaulle. He believed that France should retain Algeria, but in retirement he can have had no idea of the cancer within the French Army created by the war. However, although by 1961 sharply critical and opposed to de Gaulle's policies of extrication and withdrawal from Africa, he strongly opposed the attempted coup by four dissident generals in 1961. For him, as in 1940 to 1945, discipline, order, and respect for authority were mandatory. His views on discipline and order were also evident in his becoming honorary chairman of the Association to Defend the Memory of Marshal Pétain.

In the last fifteen years of Weygand's long life he maintained a remarkable level of physical and mental activity almost to the end. He lived in his Paris flat in the Avenue Friedland, regularly attended Académie meetings, and welcomed numerous visitors, among them personalities who had earlier been sharp critics. He scorned the lift to his fifth-floor flat, walked for at least an hour every day, and polished his own shoes and boots as befitted a cavalryman. A matter of sadness for him was that his son Jacques, despite an excellent campaign record in de Lattre's army, had been ordered to leave the army because of his Weygand name. In 1961 Renée, who had been in poor health for some time, died and was buried at Morlaix, after which Weygand went on a visit to his daughter-in-law in Ireland.

In these last years, though, his main occupation was writing, and he produced a number of works and journal articles. Most important of these were the three volumes of his *Memoirés,* volume 1, *Idéal Vécu;* volume 2, *Mirages et Réalité;* and volume 3, *Rappelé au Service.* These are factual accounts of his life written in a precise if somewhat dry style and exhibit some reticence about certain events and detail. The other important work was *En Lisant les Mémoires du Général de Gaulle,* in which he corrects a number of specific factual errors and denies the implications that de Gaulle chose to draw on his activities, particularly concerning the events of May–June 1940.[13] Weygand's rebuttals were always courteously phrased, in marked contrast to personally abusive remarks about him, his physical stature, ancestry, and field command ability made on occasions by de Gaulle, a sad vindictive streak in an otherwise towering personality. Weygand also wrote a number of short works, including forewords to the biographies or memoirs of others, Roman Catholic works, and military history. These all reflected his traditional and religious views with criticisms of political figures, and ranged from a work on Joan of Arc to kind words about the prewar years in a biography of General Dentz, the Vichy commander in Syria in 1941.

After a fall in his home from which he never recovered, Weygand died on January 28, 1965. His sons planned a memorial service at Saint-Louis-des-Invalides for the second of February at 11.00 A M. An Invalides service and memorial was his right as a general, and in Weygand's case had been specifically authorized by law in 1929. But de Gaulle was at the height of his power as president, and he flatly refused any state recognition, despite much pressure and criticism.[14] The memorial service had to be held instead at the church of Saint-Philippe de Roule. A large crowd assembled outside the church, and messages of condolences arrived from all over the world. No representative of the government was present other than a junior captain from the Ministère des Anciens Combattants, the minister himself having "other duties." No official military presence had been allowed. A large number of Second World War officers, including Marie-Pierre Koenig, *a gaulliste de la première heure,* de Monsabert, and Edouard Béthouart, were all present.

The service was taken by Cardinal Feltin, and tributes were paid by General Jean Touzet du Vigier and the director of the Académie Francaise, Jean Paulhan. In the latter tributes Paulmau unwisely made reference to "la naissance mystérieuse du général," intending this to be a contrast to Weygand's strict sense of morality, but it evoked a noisy protest from the congregation. This inappropriate remark, together with condolence messages from King Baudouin and Queen Elisabeth the queen mother of Belgium, the queen of Italy, and the heads of the dynasties of Habsburg, Orlèans, and Bourbon-Parma, led to renewed speculation concerning Weygand's parentage.

After the service was over the coffin was taken to be buried alongside that of Renée at Morlaix.

Generals who suffer disastrous defeats in major wars generally receive criticism and blame from historians. Maxime Weygand was certainly to be no exception. For many he made a convenient scapegoat, especially in times when his most bitter critic, de Gaulle, towered over his country's life. He undoubtedly made mistakes in his own life—association even if indirect with the views of right-wing groups in the 1930s, intemperate conduct in the 1940s crisis, perhaps when in North Africa not declaring for de Gaulle's Free France, the *affaire Beaufre* and the treatment of Algerian Jews, or as argued by some, even being willing to serve in the 1940 *Etat Français* in any capacity at all—although the vast majority of French officers, soldiers, and men and women of the general public were more than content to forgive them. Historians need to remember that Weygand's generation was there when the events occurred, later generations were not, and he remains one of the very few leading figures of the dismal Vichy era to emerge with real credit. Weygand's long career had to include advancing and defending unpopular policies and later making major national military decisions, in the course of which often his natural charm and kindness were lost. But most of these decisions can now be seen to have been of great value to his country, preserving its army and its honor in a country that sets great store on honor. Without the decisions made and actions set in motion by Weygand in 1940–41 in France and North Africa, the armies of Koeltz in Tunisia, of Juin in Italy, and of de Lattre de Tassigny in the liberation campaign would not have been ready to join and represent France with the Allied armies.

No one should deny that this fiery little general, temper sometimes under control but sometimes definitely not, whose only certain knowledge about his parents was that they were not French, had remained, throughout times of the most extraordinary difficulties, a passionate and devoted patriot for France.

NOTES

1. BIRTH AND EARLY YEARS, 1867–1914

1. Bernard Destremau, *Weygand* (Paris: Perrin, 1989), 17–35, provides a full account of the possible combinations. A shorter summary appears in Philip C. F. Bankwitz, *Maxime Weygand and Civil-Military Relations in Modern France* (Cambridge, Mass.: Harvard University Press, 1967), 1–8, but offers no preferred solution. Barnett Singer, in *Maxime Weygand, A Biography of the French General in Two World Wars* (Jefferson, N.C.: McFarland, 2008), asserts that the infant's parents were an Austrian Countess Zichy and the commander of the Belgian Legion of Volunteers in Mexico, Colonel Alfred van der Smissen, the countess at the time being a lady-in-waiting to Empress Charlotte. If this was true the birth must have taken place, perhaps prematurely, in 1865 and was concealed. This, together with the fact that Weygand's physical appearance suggested some part non-European parentage, makes this argument difficult to support.

2. Destremau, *Weygand*, 40–41, suggests a possibility that King Leopold or his staff may have played some part in effecting this arrangement. The evidence, however, is thin. Thérèse de Nimal always asserted that she had no knowledge of the boy's real parents.

3. Ibid., 28–48, and Spencer C. Tucker, "Maxime Weygand," in *Chief of Staff*, vol. 1: *The Principal Officers behind History's Great Commanders, Napoleonic Wars to World War I*, ed. David T. Zabecki (Annapolis: Naval Institute Press, 2008), 188–98, provide the few details available.

4. For an overview of the state of the pre-1914 French Army see Anthony Clayton, *Paths of Glory: The French Army 1914–1918* (London: Cassell, 2003).

5. Destremau, *Weygand,* 59, records this incident, the only disciplinary action taken against Weygand until the controversies of 1940. The contribution followed an emotive discussion within a group of young bachelor officers, one of whom chaffed Weygand for being richer than the others. All the contributors' names were published in a magazine; among these was Paul Valéry, the future writer and academic.

6. Ibid., 63–66, chronicles the story of the marriage. It appears that a friend, not named, advised the general that there need be no anxiety over the bridegroom's income.

7. Tucker, "Maxime Weygand," 189, notes this exceptionally rapid promotion.

8. Joffre himself later claimed that he had backed Weygand's appointment in his *Mé-moires*, vol. 1 (London: Geoffrey Bles, 1932), 286 note.

2. CHIEF OF STAFF, 1914–18

1. An excellent article by Colonel Frédéric Guelton, "Le renseignement tactique dans l'Armée Française," appears in the magazine *14–18, Le magazine de la Grande Guerre*, no. 55 (Nov./Dec./Jan. 2012): 53–59. The article recounts the development of French battlefield intelligence from the prewar thinking that cavalry would be able to support a broad out-line and anything further that was needed would be picked up in battle.

2. *Des Principes de la Guerre, Conférence Faites ā l'Ecole Supérieur de la Guerre*, and *De la Conduite de Guerre*, published in 1903 and 1905 by Berger-Levrault.

3. Countless biographies, memoirs, and other works concerned with fighting on the Western Front in general and Marshal Foch in particular fill libraries. Preparation for this work concerned with Weygand has centered on Destremau, *Weygand*, part 2, chs. 2–8, and Tucker, "Maxime Weygand." In respect of his chief, Foch, over eighty works including memoirs, analyses of his service, and opinions on his life have been published in France. A full modern biography appears in Jean-Christophe Notin, *Foch* (Paris: Perrin, 2008), a scholarly definitive work. In English, the two most important works are Elizabeth Green-halgh, *Foch in Command, The Making of a First World War General* (Cambridge: Cam-bridge University Press, 2012), and the older B. H. Liddell Hart, *Foch, The Man of Orleans* (London: Eyre and Spottiswoode, 1931), but also useful are Major General Sir George Aston, *The Biography of the Late Marshal Foch* (London: Hutchinson, 1929); Lieutenant Colonel T. M. Hunter, *Marshal Foch: A Study in Leadership* (Ottawa: Canadian Army Headquarters, 1961); Michael S. Neiberg, *Foch, Supreme Commander in the Great War* (Washington, D.C.: Brasseys, 2003) and Raymond Recouly, *Foch: His Character and Lead-ership* (London: T. Fisher Unwin, 1920).

A dissident and highly critical view of Foch that seems to belittle Weygand's work and loyalty is set out in Singer, *Maxime Weygand*, ch. 2. It represents a minority within aca-demic writing.

4. At the start of the war the French government decided to permit a small number of military chaplains, *aumoniers*, in the interest of national unity. In the event there were serving in the ranks or as noncommissioned officers a large number of men who after their compulsory national service had become monks or priests. A number, including Teilhard de Chardin, served as *brancardiers*, stretcher bearers and, irrespective of rank, acted as unofficial chaplains, celebrating Mass amid ruins and craters to those who sought it.

5. Weygand always spoke of Foch simply but devotedly as "mon chef." Destremau, *Weygand*, 96.

6. A work of French literary history is illuminating as a comparison. Martin Turnell in *The Classical Moment: Studies of Corneille, Racine and Molière* (London: Hamish Ham-ilton, 1947), 15, writes:

> The only healthy condition is a regulated tug of war. The peculiar vitality of French Literature in the Seventeenth Century lies in a very delicate poise between "reason" and "passion" in a sense of tension and response which is quite different from the tension of the English writers and which is the result of an ambient attitude towards

authority. Authority is not accepted passively. It is accepted—and—resisted, and it is this that gives the literature its life, its high degree of emotional vitality combined with a high degree of social order.

With the substitution of "generalship" for "literature" the similarity is instructive, and to become especially marked in 1918 and 1940.

7. Liddell Hart, *Foch*, 226.

8. Greenhalgh, *Foch in Command*, 141–42. The doctrine accepted that no single massive attack-type operation would be likely to succeed unless accompanied by several other simultaneous lesser attacks along the whole front. Each attack would have to be preceded and followed up by artillery fire and must not leave an enemy any opportunity to prepare a new defense.

9. Destremau, *Weygand*, 109: "Vous savez, Weygand's lorsque je me mets en colère ce n'est pas contre vous mais contre moi parce que je n'arrive pas ā me faire suffisamment comprendre bien que je sents que j'ai raison."

10. Notin, *Foch*, 229.

11. Destremau, *Weygand*, 111. "'Foch m'a encore tourneboule,' écrit Fayolle le 16 octobre. 'Heureusement j'ai vu Weygand ce matin. Les indications se présent.'"

12. Recouly, *Foch*, 12. The Belgian officer was Major de Posch, a great admirer of Foch. Brigadier the Viscount Dillon in *Memories of Three Wars* (London: Allan Wingate, 1951), part 2, also offers a good close-up account of Foch's headquarters and Weygand at work from Dillon's perspective as British Army liaison officer.

13. Destremau, *Weygand*, 114–17, quotes from Weygand's own explanation for this decision, that it would have been cowardice to have abandoned Foch at this juncture, and honor required him to stay. He must, though, have looked with some envy at the senior formation commands that many of his prewar contemporaries were now holding. Possibly he believed that Foch's abilities would soon lead to his recall to a field command. Much later de Gaulle was to observe, "Nul régiment, nulle brigade, nulle division, nul corps d'armée ne l'a vu ā sa tête."

14. Jean-Jacques Langendorf and Pierre Streit, *Face à la guerre: L'armée et le peuple suisse (1914–1918/1939–1945)* (Gollion, Switzerland: Infolio, 2007), 101–102. Greenhalgh, *Foch in Command*, 218, notes the proposed Foch command.

15. Destremau, *Weygand*, 121.

16. Ibid., 121–25. Pétain's technique appears to have been missing on this occasion as at the outset he made a disparaging remark about Foch.

17. Hunter, *Marshal Foch*, 197. The German strength had fallen to 197 divisions.

18. Destremau, *Weygand*, 134. Weygand recounted the incident to a fellow patient-detainee in 1945 in the Val-de-Grâce military hospital; his son records the words spoken.

19. Ibid., 132. At a moment of victory but irritated by Weygand's offering thanksgiving in a church and so keeping him waiting, Clemenceau exploded: "Vous devez être content. Vous avez la figure rose alors que de costume vous êtes tout jaune."

20. Maxime Weygand, *Le 11 novembre* (Paris: Flammarion, 1958).

3. VERSAILLES, WARSAW, SYRIA, 1919–24

1. Details of the post-armistice debates, with particular reference to the Foch-Clemenceau vendetta, appear in Destremau, *Weygand*, 141–45; Liddell Hart, *Foch*, ch., 23;

Margaret Macmillan, *Six Months That Changed the World* (London: John Murray, 2001), 177–81; Neiberg, *Foch*, ch. 7; and Singer, *Maxime Weygand*, ch. 3. Singer provides the source for the "quatre vieilles."

2. An article appeared in the *London Daily Mail* of April 2, 1919, in the form of an interview with Foch, endorsed by him and expressing right-wing political opinions. Weygand was accused of writing the article, an accusation that he denied. With his close association with Foch it is, however, difficult to believe that he was in no way associated with it.

3. Destremau, *Weygand*, 146, gives an example of one such an outburst. Weygand was attending a luncheon at which the French ambassador to the United States was present. During the meal the ambassador remarked on the efforts made by the United States in the war and how great a debt France owed to America. Weygand exploded, asserting that the Americans had arrived late on the scene and with many difficult logistical problems, and that it was the French Army that won the war. Embarrassment followed, and Weygand had to apologize.

4. One may speculate that Weygand's almost theatrical, deliberate positioning of himself a few steps behind Foch may have other more complex psychological reasons than that of status and loyalty. It is possible that a small element of downsizing was for him important in the service of the army, for one deep-seated reason or another, but also the downsizing may have created tensions that could account for occasional outbursts.

5. The action by the Poles was technically illegal, the Polish units at the time still being under the authority of Foch as the allied supreme commander.

6. The issue of despatching or retaining a high-profile soldier in a lost cause is interesting. President Roosevelt personally ordered General MacArthur to leave the Philippines in the face of overwhelming Japanese superiority, so denying the Japanese the triumph of his capture. Later, in 1953–54 the French government, daunted by the success of the Viet Minh, considered sending the nation's only living Marshal of France, Alphonse Juin, but decided against such an appointment, as defeat would tarnish not only the reputation of Juin but also the status of a Marshal and the prestige of the French Army. The issue should in no way be related to the physical or moral courage of the officer concerned. Juin's wider view of the question and the advice that he offered to the government appear in Bernard Pujo, *Juin, Maréchal de France* (Paris: Albin Michel, 1988), 313.

7. Henrys had unwisely accompanied the Polish Army entering Kiev, for which Paris peremptorily ordered him to return to Warsaw, but his work was already complicated by Piłsudski's dislike of the French.

8. An operational account of the Warsaw battle is given in Adam Zamoyski, *Warsaw 1920* (London: Harper Collins, 2008), though the author says little about Weygand. More details appear in Destremau, *Weygand*, 146–58; M. K. Dziewanowski, *Joseph Pilsudski: A European Federalist 1918–1932* (Stanford, Calif.: Hoover Institute, n.d. [1969]), 304–305; and Singer, *Maxime Weygand*, 51–55. I have also drawn on recollections in respect of Weygand of my late father, the British military attaché. One of the illustrations in Zamoyski's book shows officers of the French mission at work, including Weygand and the young de Gaulle, at that time an admirer of Weygand.

9. Destremau, *Weygand*, 152, records this detail.

10. Lieutenant General Sir Adrian Carton de Wiart, *Happy Odyssey* (London: Jonathan Cape, 1950), 107, records that at the time of Weygand's arrival he advised Weygand "that the issue had become entirely psychological."

11. This observation is in a letter dated May 25, 1935, from Weygand to General Jean Duval: "Je ne suis pas à l'origine du plan de bon sens conçu par l'Etat-major polonais. Mais, sans mon expérience et ma volonté agissante, l'exécution eût été lamentable." The letter, preserved by the Service Historique des Armées, is quoted in Destremau, *Weygand*, 157.

12. This interesting point is recorded in ch. 4 in Singer's *Maxime Weygand*, 308n11.

13. A number of works cover the French period in the Levant in the interwar years. Despite its age, S. H. Longrigg, *Syria and Lebanon under French Mandate* (London: Oxford University Press, 1958) remains a classic work. Also of great value is A. L. Tibawi, *A Modern History of Syria* (London: Macmillan, 1969). The story is complex, with contradictory wartime undertakings, the Turkish revival, the controversies over the areas actually to be included in the new Syria, and the hostilities between different communities all making for a difficult period in the history of the region.

14. Destremau, *Weygand*, 167–68.

4. DEFENSE POLICY IN A FRACTURED FRANCE, 1925–39

1. Eight French Army commanders were over a period of years created Marshals: Joffre and Foch during the war, Pétain immediately after its ending, the others later. These were Emile Fayolle, Louis Franchet d'Espérey, Joseph Gallieni (posthumous), Hubert Lyautey, Michel-Joseph Maunoury (posthumous). De Castelnau's last command was that of the Groupe de l'Armée de l'Est, satirized as "Groupe des Amis de l'Église," his strict Catholicism precluding a Marshal's baton despite Western Front services throughout the war and the death in action of three sons.

It is said that at the ceremony at which Pétain received his baton Weygand was heard to remark to Desticker that Pétain had acted vigorously only when kicked in the backside.

2. Destremau, *Weygand*, part 1, chs. 4 and 5 provide an account of Weygand's life in the CHEM years and the events leading up to his advancement in 1930. William Shirer, *The Collapse of the Third Republic* (London: Heinemann, 1970), books 2 and 5, gives a full overview of the politics of the years 1919 to 1939.

3. Turenne, Henri de la Tour d'Auvergne, was born into a Protestant family but converted to Roman Catholicism.

4. Weygand was, however, prone to make the occasional injudicious observation. A 1927 example is cited in Destremau, *Weygand*, 196, where in a speech at Nancy he spoke of the example of Poland's willingness to shed blood for the country's defense. Critics of Weygand seized such observations.

5. The full text is set out in ibid., 203.

6. A rich collection of Weygand's papers setting out his views and analyses of France's security problems and the controversies that they aroused at the time, together with a well-balanced commentary, appears in Frédérick Guelton, ed. *Le "Journal" du Général Weygand 1929–1935* (Montpellier: Université Paul-Valéry Montpellier III, 1998). Bankwitz, in his *Maxime Weygand and Civil-Military Relations*, develops his traditional civil-military relations case against Weygand. Destremau's perspective is in parts 4, 5, and 6 in his *Weygand*.

7. The career, policies, and thinking of General Gamelin and his influence on defense are described in detail in Martin S. Alexander, *The Republic in Danger: General Maurice Gamelin and the Politics of French Defence, 1933–1940* (Cambridge: Cambridge University Press, 1992). Taking a long-term view, Gamelin considered that France, and also Britain, would not be ready for an offensive campaign, his "Methodical Battle," before 1942. Until

then German military power would be worn down by vain attacks on the Maginot Line, and an Anglo-French naval blockade would erode civilian morale. The Poles could not be given any effective help, but a valiant Polish defense would provide cover for France's very dilatory mobilization.

8. The Ecole Supérieure de Guerre was up to 1940 still teaching that defense could be secured by a strong, well-coordinated line of fortifications, which in time would wear down the attacks of an aggressor so that after two or three years of preparation and with an Allied army three times the size of the much-reduced army of the attacker, victory would be certain. General Louis Berteil, *L'Armée de Weygand* (Paris: Albatros, 1975), 14–15.

9. Maxime Weygand, *Comment élever nos fils* (Paris: Flammarion, 1937).

10. Maxime Weygand, *La France, est elle défendue?* (Paris: Flammarion, 1937).

11. Maxime Weygand, *Histoire de l'Armée Française* (Paris: Flammarion, 1938).

12. Brian Bond, *British Military Policy between the Two World Wars* (Oxford: Clarendon, 1980), 181. The general officer commanding Southern Command, Sir John Burnett-Stuart, was very concerned over the impression the visit had left on Weygand.

13. Weygand's account of his second period of service in Syria and Lebanon is set out in his *Recalled to Service*, trans. E. W. Dickes (London: Heinemman, 1952) and Destremau, *Weygand*, 374–79. Major General R. J. Collins in *Lord Wavell 1883–1941: A Military Biography* (London: Hodder and Stoughton, 1948), 211, notes that Weygand was so impressed by Wavell that although technically the senior, he offered to serve under him if a joint Anglo-French command was created.

14. Shirer, *Collapse*, 521–23, asserts that the whole project was more the work of those who saw having a blow struck against the Soviet Union as more important than fighting Germany. This may well have been the concern of some, but Weygand's concerns from the 1920s onward had been over Germany; for him any attack on the Soviet Union (at the time an ally of Germany) was a means to an end, not an end in itself. Wavell agreed with this view.

5. COMMANDER IN CHIEF, MAY–JUNE 1940

1. Alexander, *Republic in Danger*, 323 and later 336–37, notes the origins and growth of this assessment in Gamelin's mind. In fairness to him, such an attack had been the original German plan.

2. The account of the 1940 campaign that follows focuses on Weygand's role. The context is covered in numerous accounts, of which for the purpose of this book most useful are Destremau, *Weygand*, part 7; Alistair Horne, *To Lose a Battle: France 1940* (London: Macmillan, 1969), part 2, and Weygand, *Recalled to Service*, part 2. Also providing relevant material are Bankwitz, *Maxime Weygand and Civil-Military Relations*, ch. 8; Richard Griffith, *Marshal Pétain* (London: Constable, 1970), part 3; Shirer, *Collapse*; Singer, *Maxime Weygand*, ch. 8; and Commandant Jacques Weygand, *The Role of General Weygand: Conversations with His Son*, trans. J. F. McEwen (London: Eyre and Spottiswode, 1948), chs. 2–8.

3. No aircraft had been made available for Weygand. One had to be requisitioned, its pilot demanding a real machine gun for defense in place of a wooden mock-up.

4. Postwar critics of this plan claim that Weygand was in error concentrating his effort on one section of the front, and that he should instead have planned a defense in depth further south to cover a withdrawal to North Africa. At the time, though, Weygand could hardly, as if without concern, abandon and write off the 1st Army Group, the British, and the Belgians.

5. Spears's view of Weygand verged on the racial: "Like Reynaud he looked oriental. His sparse moustache and parchment skin, his high cheek-bones protruding from a flat face shaped like an ace of spades reversed, enhanced an impression already emphasized by his very pointed chin." Major General Edward Spears, *Assignment to Catastrophe,* vol. 1: *Prelude to Dunkirk* (London: Heinemann, 1954), 183–84.

6. Writing after the war, Weygand took a more charitable view that the Belgian forces were too far from the Yser to reach the river in any time for defense, and the Belgian right flank, threatened with envelopment, could not be extricated, so leaving the king and his commanders to feel abandoned. See *Recalled to Service,* 85–86.

7. A translation of Weygand's copy of the record of this meeting is included in *Recalled to Service,* appendix 7. The specific word "armistice" was redacted from the official record, but "cessation of hostilities" appears.

8. The Italian Army and Air Force also suffered from fascist movements' interventions in their cadres. The navy was largely left alone. Its strength was a very real threat to Britain and France.

9. Bernard Ledwidge, *De Gaulle* (London: Weidenfield, 1986), 54–57, records these events.

10. Bazaine soon escaped from prison and died in exile in Spain.

6. MINISTER FOR NATIONAL DEFENSE, JUNE–SEPTEMBER 1940

1. Details of Weygand's brief period as a minister appear in Destremau, *Weygand,* part 9; Griffith, *Marshal Pétain,* part 4, ch. 2; Robert O. Paxton, *Parades and Politics at Vichy* (Princeton, N.J.: Princeton University Press, 1966), chs. 1, and 2; J. Weygand, *Role of General Weygand,* chs. 8 and 9, and Weygand, *Recalled to Service,* part 3.

2. Several visitors to Vichy, among them the United States ambassador, Admiral William D. Leahy, formed this impression.

3. Weygand, *Recalled to Service,* 246, records the creation of this intelligence service.

4. The issue remains a very real historical "might have been." With bases in Sardinia, Sicily, and the south of France and with almost certainly a permission granted by a hard-pressed General Franco for at least the passage of German troops through Spain, together with a four- or five-battleship Italian Navy together with troops in Libya, Britain could easily have been chased out of the Western Mediterranean, Gibraltar neutralized if not lost, and Malta certainly lost. British control of Egypt would have been gravely endangered. London was aware of the dangers. Steps being taken included preparations for a force of West African troops to seize a Canary island as a replacement base (troops actually embarked on ships for this) and discreet generous payments being made to certain Spanish generals and officials known to oppose extreme Falangists and advising Franco to remain neutral. Shirer, *Collapse,* 872, dismisses this contingency in two paragraphs. The first makes no mention of the Luftwaffe's ability to transport troops and equipment by air and seize airfields. The second quotes General Halder as saying that the German Army could not keep invasion of England and an assault on French North Africa as priorities. The Germans would have been wiser to opt for North Africa.

7. A GENERAL OUT OF STEP

1. The arguments are well summarized with excerpts from documents in Bankwitz, *Maxime Weygand,* 330–44. An argument even more stretched, put forward by some, held

that Weygand's policy served German interests as his ruse defended North Africa against a British or American seaborne invasion. But America entered the war only after Weygand's recall, and Britain, with resources already stretched and with war clouds looming in the Far East, was in no position to mount an effective invasion. Nor was Germany, preparing for the invasion of the Soviet Union and then attacking, in a state ready for a major North Africa campaign. All these factors would have been known to Weygand. Bankwitz seems to suggest that Weygand's rebuilding of an army in North Africa was either unnecessary or simply a means to keep de Gaulle out. All such argument, of which there was to be more after the end of the war, appears political and certainly does not accord with Weygand's real aims and achievements.

2. Darlan's world-stage appreciation and his views regarding Weygand's opposition are set out in Hervé Couteau-Bégarie and Claude Huan, *Darlan* (Paris: Fayard, 1989), ch. 15.

3. The question is glossed over in Destremau, *Weygand*, 668–70, and is covered in fuller measure in Singer, *Maxime Weygand*, 141–48. Robert Ageron, *Modern Algeria*, trans. Michael Brett (London: Hurst, 1964), 98, notes the pleasure of the Algerian French settlers.

4. Weygand's relations with Murphy are usefully set out in his *Recalled to Service*, 368–78, and in Robert Murphy, *Diplomat among Warriors* (London: Collins, 1964), 123–26.

5. Goums were semiregular Moroccan company-sized subunits. A goum traditionally totaled some 200 goumiers, of which 120 were foot soldiers, 50 on horse or pony back, and a mule support section. Some goums, at various times, had an additional machine gun section.

6. A very full account of this mutiny is set out in Berteil, *L'Armée de Weygand*, 87–91. Berteil, later a general, was serving as a Zouave infantry officer at the time. He notes the German propaganda was anti-Semitic and promised the end of French rule in Algeria. Financial incentives were also offered.

7. Weygand, *Recalled to Service*, 197–98, provides these totals.

8. Paxton, *Parades and Politics*, 200, provides a table showing both sets of figures.

9. Berteil, *L'Armée de Weygand*, 73, names the Royal Navy light cruiser HMS *Aurora*, one of two or three light cruisers, which with a few powerful destroyers formed the navy's Force K based at Malta.

10. Paxton, *Parades and Politics*, 228, and Singer, *Maxime Weygand*, 169–70, outline this event. Destremau makes no mention of it in his *Weygand*. Beaufre had an almost legendary military career commencing with being badly wounded, stripped, and left for dead in the Rif War, then in the Second World War campaigns, Indochina, Suez in 1956, and finishing with a senior command in the Algerian war.

11. The passions and the heat of the exchanges in these talks is well conveyed in Destremau, *Weygand*, 685–92, and Weygand's *Recalled to Service*, 326–36.

12. The text of this instruction is printed in full in General René Chambe, *Le Maréchal Juin, duc du Garigliano* (Paris: Plon, 1983), 112–14. Unwisely a copy was sent to Vichy, where it caused near panic in the fear that the Germans might learn of it. Juin was rebuked and ordered to have all copies burned. But several copies were secretly retained, and the spirit of the order was followed.

13. By custom, the officer cadets of the Saint-Cyr military academy were allowed to choose the name for their intake *promotion* after their first year. In the summer of 1942 a delegation from the 1941 entry opted for *Promotion Général Weygand* as their choice. The

choice was disallowed as men still living were not permitted. Instead the cadets chose the name of Charles Foucauld, a one-time army officer who became a strict Catholic monk, lived in the Sahara as a missionary, and was murdered there. This second choice of the *promotion* carried equally clear political undertones. The event was gratifying for the strictly Catholic Weygand, although after the war in an academic context amid private conversation he was to criticize Foucauld's theological teaching.

8. FINAL MISFORTUNES AND FINAL YEARS, 1941–65

1. Destremau, *Weygand*, 711–12. The remark should not be viewed as simply a veiled attack on de Gaulle.

2. Destremau, *Weygand*, 716–29, and Weygand himself in *Recalled to Service*, 390–92, record the visit. The United States was of course now at war, but not with Vichy France.

3. Pétain recounted a story of a visit that he made with Admiral Darlan to Toulon where he himself was cheered by crowds. At one quieter point in the cheering a voice shouted out "Vive Darlan." Pétain turned to the admiral and remarked caustically "So you are a ventriloquist, Darlan." Weygand, *Recalled to Service*, p. 394.

4. The accounts of those early November events are as confusing as the events themselves. Of use are Couteau-Bégarie and Huan, *Darlan*, chs. 19 and 20; Destremau, *Weygand*, 726–37; Griffith, *Marshal Pétain*, 307–15; Jacques Weygand, *Conversations*, 181–82, and Weygand, *Recalled to Service*, 397–403.

5. Whether the presence of Laval and the police secretary-general at Weygand's farewell had any connection with his arrest a few hours later after delays in departure is unknown. Weygand himself believed that it was unlikely and that Laval and the police officer were there to warn him of the degree of the distrust in which he was held by the Germans. Pétain felt a personal responsibility and blamed himself.

6. Weygand's time and experience in German detention are described in Destremau, *Weygand*, 732–43. Bankwitz, *Maxime Weygand and Civil-Military Relations,* 354n69, adds that Hitler and Himmler saw Weygand as a useful hostage and that other plots against him were thwarted by the anti-Nazi Abwehr chief, Admiral Canaris.

7. The arrival of the Weygands at Lindau is described in Major-General Sir Guy Salisbury-Jones, *So Full a Glory: A Biography of Marshal de Lattre de Tassigny* (London: Weidenfeld, 1954), 207–208, and Destremau, *Weygand*, 744–49.

8. The inclusion of France was so late a decision that, as no French flag was to hand for the ceremony at Karlshorst, one had to be hurriedly stitched together from old clothes and a sheet.

9. Pétain was convicted and sentenced to death. The sentence was commuted to life imprisonment on account of his age. He spent the last six years of his life in an island fortress prison, his faculties declining. He died in July 1951. His only last wish, to be buried at Verdun with his soldiers, was denied him.

10. This account of the proceedings of the High Court and the commission is a summary of the detail set out in Destremau, *Weygand*, 750–65; Jules Roy, *Le Grand Naufrage* (Paris: Juillard, 1966), translated as *The Trial of Marshal Pétain* by Robert Baldick (London: Faber and Faber, 1968) and later republished under the title of *Blows at the Trial of Pétain*, 85–88, 92–100, and Singer, *Maxime Weygand*, 177–85.

11. Weygand did not specifically mention a fault line, but this view appears to complement the theory advanced in this work.

12. The details of these proceedings appear in Chambe, *Le Maréchal Juin*, ch. 17, which includes facsimiles of letters from Juin and Weygand. In the event the title was conferred on Juin, and posthumously on de Lattre, who, dying from cancer, was made aware that the honor was to be conferred. Generals Leclerc and, later, Koenig were both made Marshals posthumously. Juin remained to be France's last living Marshal, a sad figure who was to be deprived of almost all his privileges as a Marshal following his opposition to de Gaulle's Algerian policies. Later the two old men, veterans of the same Saint-Cyr *promotion,* were reconciled.

13. All three volumes were published by Flammarion in Paris, in 1953, 1957, and 1960 respectively. *En Lisant les Mémoires du Général de Gaulle* was published in 1955, also by Flammarion.

14. Destremau, *Weygand,* 773–82, recounts this unhappy story. Philippe de Gaulle, *De Gaulle, Mon Pére: Entretiens avec Michel Tauriac* (Paris: Plon, 2003), 104, states the reason for de Gaulle's decision was that Weygand had never won a victory.

SELECTED BIBLIOGRAPHY

Ageron, Robert. *Modern Algeria.* Trans. Michael Brett. London: Hurst, 1964.

Alexander, Martin S. *The Republic in Danger: General Maurice Gamelin and the Politics of French Defence, 1933–1940.* Cambridge: Cambridge University Press, 1992.

Alexander, Martin S., and William J. Philpott, eds. *Anglo-French Defence Relations between the Wars.* Basingstoke: Palgrave Macmillan, 2002.

Ash, Bernard. *A Biography of the Field Marshal Sir Henry Wilson.* London: Cassel, 1965.

Aston, George. *The Biography of the Late Marshal Foch.* London: Hutchinson, 1929.

Auphan, Paul, and Jacques Mordal. *The French Navy in World War II.* Trans. Captain A. C. J. Sabalot. Annapolis, Md.: United States Naval Institute, 1959.

Bankwitz, Philip C. F. *Maxime Weygand and Civil-Military Relations in Modern France.* Cambridge, Mass.: Harvard University Press, 1967.

Berteil, Louis. *L'Armée de Weygand,* Paris: Albatros, 1975.

Bond, Brian. *British Military Policy between the Two World Wars.* Oxford: Clarendon, 1980.

Bonham-Carter, Victor. *Soldier True: The Life and Times of Field Marshal Sir William Robertson.* London: Frederick Miller, 1963.

Calwell, C. G. *Field Marshal Sir Henry Wilson.* Vol. 2. London: Cassell, 1927.

Carton de Wiart, Adrian. *Happy Odyssey.* London: Jonathan Cape, 1950.

Chambe, René. *Le Maréchal Juin, duc du Garigliano.* Paris: Plon, 1983.

Churchill, Winston, S. *The Second World War.* Vol. 2: *Their Finest Hour.* London: Cassell, 1948.

Chuter, David. *Humanity's Soldier: France and International Security, 1919–2001.* Providence, R.I.: Bergham, 1996.

Clayton, Anthony. *Three Marshals of France.* London: Brassey's, 1992.

———. *Paths of Glory: The French Army 1914–1918.* London: Cassell, 2003.

Cobban, Alfred. *A History of Modern France.* Vol. 3: *1871–1962.* London: Penguin, 1965.

Collins, R. J. *Lord Wavell 1883–1941: A Military Biography.* London: Hodder and Stoughton, 1948.

Colville, J. R. *Man of Valour: The Life of Field Marshal the Viscount Gort.* London: Collins, 1972.

Cooper, Duff. *Haig*. London: Faber, 1935.

Couteau-Bégarie, Hervé, and Claude Huan. *Darlan*. Paris: Fayard, 1989.

Dallas, George. *At the Heart of a Tiger: Clemenceau and His World*. London: Macmillan, 1993.

Destremau, Bernard. *Weygand*. Paris: Perrin, 1989.

Dillon, Eric FitzGerald. *Memories of Three Wars*. London: Allan Wingate, 1951.

Dziewanowski, M. K. *Joseph Pilsudski: A European Federalist 1918–1932*. Stanford, Calif.: Hoover Institution Press, n.d. [1969].

Ferro, Marc. *Pétain*. Paris: Fayard, 1987.

Foch, Ferdinand. *De La Conduite de Guerre*. Paris: Berger-Levrault, 1905.

———. *Des Principes de la Guerre: Conférences Faites ā L'Ecole Supérieure de la Guerre*. Paris: Berger-Levrault, 1903.

Fraser, David. *Alanbrooke*. London: Collins, 1982.

Gamelin, M. *Servir*. 3 vols. Paris: Plon, 1947.

Gaulle, Charles de. *Mémoires*. 3 vols. Paris: Plon, 1954, 1956, 1959.

Gaulle, Philippe de. *De Gaulle, Mon Pére: Entretiens avec Michel Tauriac*. Paris: Plon, 2003.

Greenhalgh, Elizabeth. *Foch in Command: The Making of a First World War General*. Cambridge: Cambridge University Press, 2012.

Griffith, Richard. *Marshal Pétain*. London: Constable, 1970.

Grigg, John. *Lloyd George: War Leader 1916–1918*. London: Penguin, 2003.

Guelton, Frédéric. *Le "Journal" du Général Weygand, 1929–1935*. Montpellier: Université Paul-Valery Montpellier III, 1998.

———. "Le renseignement tactique dans l'Armée Française." *14–18 Le magazine de la Grande Guerre*, no. 55 (Nov./Dec./Jan. 2012): 53–59.

Harris, J. P. *Douglas Haig and the First World War*. Cambridge: Cambridge University Press, 2008.

Horne, Alistair. *The French Army in Politics 1870–1970*. London: Macmillan, 1984.

———. *To Lose a Battle: France 1940*. London: Macmillan, 1969.

Hunter, T. M. *Marshal Foch: A Study in Leadership*. Ottawa: Canadian Army Headquarters, 1961.

Joffre, Maréchal Joseph. *Mémoires*. Vol. 1. Paris: Plon, 1932.

———. *The Memoirs of Marshal Joffre*. Trans. T. Bentley Mott. London: Geoffrey Bles, 1932.

Kedward, H. R. *Occupied France: Collaboration and Resistance 1940–1944*. Oxford: Basil Blackwell, 1985.

Langendorf, Jean-Jacques, and Pierre Streit. *Face à la guerre: L'armée et le peuple suisse (1914–1918/1939–1945)*. Gollion, Switzerland: Infolio, 2007.

Ledwidge, Bernard. *De Gaulle*. London: Weidenfeld, 1986.

Liddell Hart, B. H. *Foch, The Man of Orleans*. London: Eyre and Spottiswoode, 1931.

Longrigg, S. H. *Syria and Lebanon under French Mandate*. London: Oxford University Press, 1958.

Macleod, Roderick, and Denis Kelly, eds. *The Ironside Diaries*. London: Constable, 1962.

Macmillan, Margaret. *Six Months That Changed the World*. London: John Murray, 2001.

Murphy, Robert. *Diplomat among Warriors*. London: Collins, 1964.

Neiberg, Michael S. *Foch, Supreme Commander in the Great War*. Washington, D.C.: Brassey's, 2003.

Notin, Jean-Christophe. *Foch*. Paris: Perrin, 2008.

Paxton, Robert O. *Parades and Politics at Vichy*. Princeton, N.J.: Princeton University Press, 1966.

Pershing, John J. *My Experiences in the World War*. London: Hodder and Stoughton, 1931.

Pujo, Bernard. *Juin, Maréchal de France*. Paris: Albin Michel, 1988.

Recouly, Raymond. *Foch: His Character and Leadership*. London: T. Fisher Unwin, 1920.

Reynaud, Paul. *Au Coeur de la Melée*. Paris: Flammarion, 1951.

———. *La France a sauvé l'Europe*. Paris: Flammarion, 1947.

Robertson, William. *From Private to Field Marshal*. London: Constable, 1921.

Roy, Jules. *The Trial of Marshal Pétain*. Trans. Robert Baldick. London: Faber and Faber, 1968.

Salisbury-Jones, Guy. *So Full a Glory: A Biography of Marshal de Lattre de Tassigny*. London: Weidenfeld, 1954.

Schofield, Victoria. *Wavell, Soldier and Statesman*. London: John Murray, 2006.

Serman, William, and Jean-Paul Bertaud. *Nouvelle Histoire Militaire de la France 1789–1919*. Paris: Fayard, 1996.

Shirer, William L. *The Collapse of the Third Republic*. London: Heinemann, 1970.

Singer, Barnett. *Maxime Weygand: A Biography of the French General in Two World Wars*. Jefferson, N.C.: McFarland, 2008.

Smythe, Donald. *Pershing, General of the Armies*. Bloomington: Indiana University Press, 1986.

Spears, Edward. *Assignment to Catastrophe*. Vol. 1: *Prelude to Dunkirk*. London: Heinemann, 1954.

Tibawi, A. L. *A Modern History of Syria*. London: Macmillan, 1969.

Tucker, Spencer C. "Maxime Weygand." In *Chief of Staff*, vol. 1: *The Principal Officers behind History's Great Commanders, Napoleonic Wars to World War I*, ed. David T. Zabecki, 188–98. Annapolis: Naval Institute Press, 2008.

Weygand, Jacques. *The Role of General Weygand: Conversations with His Son*. Trans. J. F. McEwen. London: Eyre and Spottiswoode, 1948.

Weygand, Maxime. *Comment élever nos fils*. Paris: Flammarion, 1937.

———. *En Lisant les Mémoires du Général de Gaulle*. Paris: Flammarion, 1957.

———. *Histoire de l'Armée Française*. Paris: Flammarion, 1938.

———. *La France, est-elle défendue?* Paris: Flammarion, 1937

———. *Le Maréchal Foch*. Paris: Flammarion, 1929.

———. *Le 11 novembre*. Paris: Flammarion, 1958.

———. *Mémoires*. Vol. 1: *Idéal Vécu*. Paris: Flammarion, 1953.

———. *Mémoires*. Vol. 2: *Mirages et Réalité*. Paris: Flammarion, 1957.

———. *Mémoires*. Vol. 3: *Rappelé au Service*. Paris: Flammarion, 1950.

———. *Recalled to Service*. Trans. E. W. Dickes. London: Heinemann, 1952.

———. *Turenne*. Paris: Flammarion, 1929.

Wheeler-Bennett, John. *The Nemesis of Power: The German Army in Politics 1918–1945, with a New Introduction by Richard Overy*. Basingstoke, U.K.: Palgrave Macmillan, 2005.

Zabecki, David T., ed. *Chief of Staff*. Vol. 1: *The Principal Officers behind History's Great Commanders, Napoleonic Wars to World War I*. Annapolis: Naval Institute Press, 2008.

Zamoyski, Adam. *Warsaw 1920*. London: HarperCollins, 2008.

INDEX

Abrial, Jean, 84, 124
Aubrac, Lucien, 137

Baudouin, Paul, 111
Béthouart, Edouard, 140
Billotte, Gaston, 82–85
Blanchard, Georges, 83, 85–86
Bliss, Tasker, 33
Blum, Léon, 69, 72–73, 118
Boisson, Pierre, 116, 126
Boncour, Joseph Paul-, 65
Bonfils, Abbé de, 6
Bonnet, Georges, 73
Borotra, Jean, 133–35
Briand, Aristide, 57–58, 60, 63
Brooke, Alan, 96
Buhrer, Jules, 87

Cadorna, Luigi, 33
Carton de Wiart, Adrian, 49
Castelnau, Edouard de, 22–24, 26,
     28–30, 147
Catroux, Georges, 107, 112, 124
Chautemps, Camille, 64, 67, 98, 100
Chiefs of staff, duties of, 16
Churchill, Winston, 39, 84–85, 87, 90,
     94–95, 120, 124, 129
Clayton, Emilius, 49
Clemenceau, Georges, 16, 28, 33–35, 38–39,
     42–44, 46, 62

Clemenceau, Michel, 133
Cohen, David, 4–5, 7–8
Combes, Emile, government 1902–1905, 9
Command styles, British and French com-
     pared, 18–19
Condé, Charles, 108
Corap, André, 83

Dakar, September 1940, 113, 115–16, 121,
     125–26
Daladier, Edouard, 65, 67–68, 75–77, 133
Darlan, François, 76, 87, 98, 107, 111, 113, 117,
     124–27, 130
Decoux, Jean, 112
de Gaulle, Charles, 112–14, 116–17, 119,
     124–26, 128–30, 134–40
de Monsabert, Joseph Goislard, 137, 140
de la Porte du Theil, Joseph, 132
de la Rocque, Casimir, 63, 66, 68, 133
de Lattre de Tassigny, Jean, 68, 134, 141
de Nimal, Thérèse, 4, 5–6
Dentz, Henri, 126–27, 139
des Portes, Hélène, 82, 95
Desticker, Pierre-Henry, 20
Doumenc, André, 78, 82–83, 93
Dreyfus affair, xii, 8–10, 29, 44, 46, 62

Faisal I (king), 52
Fayolle, Emile, 28, 45
Feltin, Maurice (cardinal), 140

Foch, Ferdinand, 16–17; pre-1914 war, 9; in 1914, 12–13, 16–24; in 1915, 24–26; in 1916, 27–30; in 1917, 30–33; 1918 fighting, 33–43; Armistice, 43–44; at Versailles, 45–47; death, 59
French, John, 19, 22–24

Gamelin, Maurice, 13, 61, 64–66, 71–72, 75–76, 78–80, 82, 133, 137
Gasser, Roger, 53, 79, 128
Georges, Alphonse, 78–80, 88, 91, 93–94, 107
Gide, André, 109
Giraud, 83
Gort, John, 83–86
Gouraud, Henri, 51–52
Guillaumat, Adolphe, 62

Haig, Douglas, 19, 24, 27, 32, 36–38, 40, 42–43
Henrys, Paul, 48, 51
Herriot, Edouard, 53, 57–58, 64–66, 105
Huntziger, Charles, 83, 90, 93–94, 102, 105–106, 111, 113, 117, 122, 125, 127

Joffre, Joseph: before 1914, 12; 1914–16, 13, 19, 20–29, 33–34, 73, 81
Juin, Alphonse, 55, 122, 127, 138, 141

Keyes, Roger, 84
Koeltz, Louis, 86, 122, 141

Lanrezac, Charles, 19
Lebanon, 51–54, 75, 99. See also Syria and Lebanon
Lebrun, Albert, 67, 87, 99–100, 104, 136
Lemaigre-Dubreuil, Jacques, 125
Leopold III (king), 83–84
Lindbergh, Charles, 105
Lloyd George, David, 32–33, 39, 46, 48
Loustaunau-Lacau, Georges, 125
Ludendorff, Erich, 36, 41
Lyautey, Hubert, 17, 56–57, 68, 119

Maginot, André, 47, 51, 60, 67–69
Maginot Line, 58, 64–65, 73, 77–79, 88–89, 106, 108

Massigli, René, 130
Maud'huy, Louis, 22
Maximilian I (archduke and emperor), 4
McAuliffe, Anthony, 134
Mers el-Kébir, 103; June 1940, 111, 115, 121, 124
Murphy, Robert J., 120

Nivelle, Robert, 28–32
Noguès, Charles, 107, 119

Orlando, Vittorio, 46

Painlevé, Paul, 33, 57–59, 68
Paulhan, Jean, 140
Pershing, John, 38, 42–43
Pétain, Philippe, x, 10, 26, 28, 32–40, 42–43, 55, 57, 59–61, 65–66, 68, 70, 80–81, 84, 87–91, 93, 98–106, 108–14, 117–18, 122, 124, 126–27, 129–32, 135–38
Peyrouton, Marcel, 118
Pilsudski, Josef, 47–50
Plan 17, 10
Platon, 131
Poincaré, Henri, 51, 68
Poland, in 1920, 47–50
Prételat, Andre-Gaston, 90–91

Reynaud, Paul, 76, 79–80, 82, 84–89, 93–100, 107, 133–36
Ribbentrop, Joachim von, 132
Robertson, William, 18, 31–32
Roosevelt, Franklin, 100, 128–29
Rundstedt, Gerd von, 131

Saget, Madame, 5
Sarrail, Maurice, 26, 54
Sarraut, Albert, 65
Serre, Charles, 137
Sidi, Mohammed V., 119
Spears, Edward, 26, 85–86, 100
Sprecher von Bernegg, Théophile, 30
Syria and Lebanon: in the 1920s, 51–54; 1939–40, 75–76, 122, 125–26, 139

Tedder, 134
Tukhachevsky, Mikhail, 47, 49

Van Overstraeten, Raoul, 84

Vuillemin, Joseph, 78, 86–87

Wavell, Archibald, 75, 80, 117

Weygand, Edouard, 13, 59, 71, 135

Weygand, Francis-Joseph, 8

Weygand, Jacques, 59, 71, 89, 128, 130, 133, 139

Weygand, Maxime: birth and ancestry, 2–4; upbringing, 5–7; Catholic teaching, 5–7; Saint-Cyr, 7–8; as a young officer, 8–13; marriage, 11–12; immediate pre-1914 years, 12–13; selected as chief of staff, 13; August–December 1914, 16–24; in 1915, 24–26; in 1916, 26–30; in 1917, 30–34; January–October 1918, 34–43; armistice and Versailles, 43–47; in Poland, 47–50; in Syria, 51–54; defense policy 1925–40, 55–76; commander in chief May–June 1940, 77–101; minister for defense 1940, 102–14; commander in chief, Africa, 115–27

Weygand, Renée, 11, 53, 58, 115, 128, 131, 133–34, 139–40

Wilson, Henry, 16, 24, 27, 33, 39, 51

Wilson, Woodrow, 43, 46, 47

ANTHONY CLAYTON is a retired official of the British Colonial Government of Kenya, former senior lecturer at the Royal Military Academy, Sandhurst, and former associate lecturer at the University of Surrey. He is author of sixteen books, including *Paths of Glory: The French Army, 1914–1918*; *The British Officer: Leaders of the Army from 1660s to the Present*; *Defeat: When Nations Lose a War*; and *Warfare in Woods and Forests* (IUP, 2012).